STATISTICS MADE SIMPLE FOR SCHOOL LEADERS

Data-Driven Decision Making

Susan Rovezzi Carroll
David J. Carroll

A SCARECROWEDUCATION BOOK
PUBLISHED IN PARTNERSHIP WITH THE AMERICAN
ASSOCIATION OF SCHOOL ADMINISTRATORS

The Scarecrow Press, Inc.
Lanham, Maryland, and Oxford
2002

A SCARECROWEDUCATION BOOK

PUBLISHED IN PARTNERSHIP WITH
THE AMERICAN ASSOCIATION OF SCHOOL ADMINISTRATORS

Published in the United States of America
by Scarecrow Press, Inc.
A Member of the Rowman & Littlefield Publishing Group
4720 Boston Way, Lanham, Maryland 20706
www.scarecroweducation.com

PO Box 317
Oxford
OX2 9RU, UK

British Library Cataloguing in Publication Information Available

Library of Congress Cataloging-in-Publication Data

Carroll, Susan Rovezzi.
    Statistics made simple for school leaders : data-driven decision making /
Susan Rovezzi Carroll, David J. Carroll.
        p. cm.
    "A ScarecrowEducation book."
    "Published in partnership with the American Association of
School Administrators."
    Includes bibliographical references and index.
    ISBN 0-8108-4481-8 (alk. paper)–ISBN 0-8108-4322-6 (pbk. : alk. paper)
    1. Educational statistics. 2. School managment and organization–
United States. I. Carroll, David J., 1953- II. Title.

LB2846 .C33 2002
370'.21–dc21   2002070569

DEDICATION

Written in the shadow of September 11, 2001, it is fitting that this book is dedicated to those who can shape the future of this world.

First, to Annie Lennon Carroll: may her love of life and tolerance of others find expression in her films. And to Mary Grace Calafiore: may her intelligence and compassion help to lead others toward a vision of peace.

This book is also dedicated to a group of children we hold dear to our hearts: our niece Rebecca Rovezzi, Olivia Matarese, Loren and Kenzie Nudelman, Emily and Ellen French, Julia Olsen, Seth Durette, Racheal Polinsky, and the Magistrali girls. May your footprints create a path toward a gentle-hearted world.

CONTENTS

FOREWORD

One of the greatest challenges facing school system leaders today is harnessing the power of data to drive school improvement. In the wake of recent federal legislation, districts are scrambling to gather data on every student on a variety of levels and to use that data to promote higher achievement.

Unfortunately, just having the data isn't enough. As one superintendent recently said, "We have lots of data—but not much information." The problem is not just having data, but also understanding the issues data illuminates—and equally important, what it does not or cannot reveal. Increasingly, school system leaders are called upon to explain their data to the public, the school board, the state, and even the federal government; this requires a thorough understanding of what data means. Understanding the limitations and significance of data is crucial to using data for school improvement; the underpinning for this analysis is a good understanding of statistics.

Statistics Made Simple for School Leaders lays out, in simple English, the fundamentals that every school system leader should know: what questions can you ask of your data, how do you determine whether changes in data are significant, how do you determine relationships between various data points, and how do you report data in a comprehensible manner to the public and the school board.

Statistics Made Simple for School Leaders is a reference that all school system leaders will find helpful in the accomplishment of their daily challenges.

Paul D. Houston, Ph.D.
Executive Director
American Association of School Administrators

Introduction

DATA RICH AND INFORMATION POOR: MAKING THE TRANSITION

Data-driven decision making is a rapidly evolving and dynamic trend. It has the potential to influence public education beyond any public school reform initiative that has yet been designed. Savvy educational leaders are beginning to use data-based technology to profile student performance, achievement trends, curricula and program changes, staffing needs, space and resource allocation, and fiscal expenditures. They are also using this technology to make choices concerning effective instructional methods, academic interventions, student behavior strategies, and management approaches intended to impact their schools in positive ways. The options for collecting, aggregating, and interpreting data for use in initiatives for school improvement are steadily increasing. It is no wonder that educators have begun to talk about the value of "data warehousing" and "mining the data."

Historically, public schools have had access to volumes of data, including standardized test scores, individualized student records, and the records of professional development of teachers and other staff. Despite this wealth of data, decision making in school districts, at best, has been based on frequency counts of raw data or on the averaging of standardized test scores on the aggregate level. At worst, it has relied on hunches and best guesses. The data were rarely used to assess the quality of learning and teaching occurring at the school or classroom level. At the same time, educators have been increasingly called on to improve student performance and be accountable to taxpayers, students, parents, government officials, and the business community. To be responsive to their stakeholders, school districts have been struggling to align the reporting of their data with information expectations.

Two major factors have constrained educators from making the most effective use of the valuable data at their disposal. The first involved the lack of a system that could attack the colossal data sources, organize the data, and sort the information into a system that could be accessible and friendly to school administrators. To say that the data available in virtually any school district could be characterized as unwieldy and disparate is an understatement.

Fortunately, the advent of user-friendly software and World Wide Web–based products gave educators the wherewithal to install data collection systems that met information needs and were able to generate data-warehousing opportunities. Some programs were very expensive; some were free. Some were limited to counting numbers for frequencies, while others were virtually limitless in their statistical capabilities (bordering on the esoteric). Some schools developed their own customized data management systems. All of these approaches made it possible for school districts to make the transition from being data rich and information poor; they were on the fast track toward becoming data driven.

Educational leaders are beginning to find themselves at the controls of data warehouses that are jam-packed with standardized test scores, Scholastic Aptitude Test (SAT) results, assessments of reading and math literacy, faculty and staff profiles, demographic and enrollment data, classroom performance assessments, and student behavior and attendance records. These data warehouses can be "massaged" to produce a host of statistics with just the click of the computer mouse. In fact, the term *data mining* has become commonly accepted jargon for the application of statistical techniques to school data. However, the popularity of data warehousing and data mining has exposed a raw nerve. With the zeal to embrace data-driven decision making, the presence of a second inhibiting factor has been uncovered—statistics anxiety. The lack of comfort that many educators have in working with statistics poses a great challenge as school districts make the transition into an information-rich environment.

Many educational leaders feel uncertain and uneasy about statistical procedures, statistical analysis, and the interpretation of results. Their graduate school classes in research design and statistics were mathematically difficult, were highly technical, and, perhaps most importantly, lacked real application to the issues they encountered on the job. Statistics became synonymous with innumerable calculations and the memorization of formulas.

Not surprising, statistics at the district and building levels has been approached with trepidation. To some extent, the software technology and statistical packages have provided a new automobile but no course in driver's education. Without a basic knowledge of statistics, the use of statistical software and data management technology can provide schools with misinformation that can have serious consequences.

There are three areas in which some educational leaders lack requisite skills:

1. The ability to frame questions so that the data can be aggregated and disaggregated to provide answers
2. The knowledge to select the right statistical procedures to answer the questions
3. The awareness of how the statistical techniques operate in a conceptual sense

Certainly, educators know what questions they want answered. They cover the gamut:

- What does tracking our standardized scores indicate about student performance?
- To what are school attendance patterns related?
- How are seniors performing on SATs for optimal college acceptance?
- Are the new reading textbooks increasing the performance of at-risk students?
- Has our behavior management program had an impact on discipline in our schools?
- Which remedial program is a better investment?

- How much effect has the new mathematics curriculum had on student achievement?
- Why is the referral rate to special education increasing?
- What is the impact of extracurricular activities on student performance?

Yet, answering these fundamental statistical questions remains a mystery for some:

- Why should you report standard deviation along with a mean score?
- What type of *t*-test do you need to answer your important questions?
- When is the median a more useful and accurate statistic?
- Why does your ANOVA report incomplete information?
- Can you calculate a mean with nominal data?
- Why should you choose a probability level of .01 instead of .05?
- Why should you downplay statistical significance in your correlation coefficient?
- When should you use a chi square analysis?

Educational leaders will need basic skills and at least a minimum level of expertise to transform their vast data warehouses into powerhouses of information delivery. To do this, they will need to use statistics correctly, judiciously, and strategically.

The purpose of this book is to help educational leaders make the transition from being data rich to information rich. This book is intended to be a user-friendly practitioner's primer, presenting the basics of what you need to know. It is in no way intended as a statistical textbook. There are no complicated mathematical formulas inside its covers. Rather, it presents basic statistical concepts in a simple, conceptual, and immediately applicable manner. It is intended to take the mystery out of the field of statistics and make it accessible to educators so that they can shake the intimidation and overwhelming feeling that it unfortunately engenders.

By focusing on conceptual application versus statistical theory, this book will leave the reader with the confident attitude that "I can do this," making statistics an enjoyable tool that will benefit educational leaders, their schools, and stakeholders. In the long run, this book is intended to underscore the magnificence of data-driven decisions. Decisions based on excellent data input, management, analysis, and interpretation produce meaningful action strategies that benefit the school and all of its stakeholders, including students, parents, educators, and the community.

THE VALUE OF GETTING INTIMATE WITH YOUR DATA

Statistics is an academic course that few educational leaders look forward to taking. Usually, there is a large gap between a high school math course and a graduate course of study. First, for many, math was one of the least-favorite courses in high school. Often, it was taken because it was a college application requirement. Second, there is little understanding of what exactly statistics is. The image is that this field of study is formula driven, intricately complex, and downright intimidating. Finally, faculty members who emphasize the computational process of calculating statistics teach many statistical courses in college. This reinforces the negative image and further alienates students from pursuing graduate-level study that includes this important and useful field.

This book is not a statistics text. It is a primer for educational leaders who want to use statistics to help them fully understand their schools, their programs, and their stakeholders, whether they are students and their families, the entire school staff, or the community at large. Statistics is a powerful management tool for school leaders. When based on hard data, strategic decisions can be made with confidence and conviction.

In this book, statistics is presented as a way of thinking. It is a logical, simplified way of using data to present information in a strategic manner. We hope the discussion will present the enormous benefits of embracing statistics. The result will be educational leaders who can communicate effectively with impact and with fortitude as they persevere to make smart, data-driven decisions.

STATISTICS

Look at the data set in figure 1.1, which represents pre- and post-performance test scores for 28 students. It can make your head spin. What can you tell about overall student performance from "eyeballing" the data set?

- Are most children performing well or poorly?
- What is the typical score for the majority of students?
- Were the instructional techniques you employed this year effective?
- If students are making gains, to what degree is this happening?
- Are students from different classrooms performing the same?
- Are segments of students (boys and girls) performing differently?
- How does performance compare with other schools in the system or the region?

Most of us cannot answer these questions by looking at a set of data. Even the small set of 28 pre-performance and post-performance scores displayed in the figure is incomprehensible. Our human minds are limited in the capacity to absorb a huge set of numbers, retain them, process them, and then make sense of them in interpretation.

Statistics is an area of mathematics that seeks to make order out of a diverse collection of facts. With a single number, statistics can summarize the properties of large groups of numbers. By using these techniques, we are able to crunch large sets of numbers into usable and "actionable" information.

If you have been given a massive assortment of numbers and have no hope of understanding them, although you have looked at them for hours, use statistics. Life will be simple. How great is that?

```
001 2221222132111211201021202011102011111210122011221011
001 3120121112312020011111111013111121052201
002 131111313111230030111311311110133312132111110110110
002 1010132111211010111011011111121052211
003 322132213221221020202110302120200120021031200020011
003 2030121002312021012111201221120952101
004 333033312330032000203220302130300120021010300030003
004 30300300033030300020133003301121052001
005 22112213232112112011221121231121112202123120112111111
005 1131121111013121112311111121102115211
006 1221122111111121121112121211111101111021111100121111
006 11200220020010201121112112101111105320
007 2221222123311210203211313011312002101211212000310211
007 30211221222120211110112012211111052211
008 2211221112210211101122212012112101211211311010211122
008 102122111221202111231221122211120952101
009 333133212321022031002130302130203130033030300032003
009 3032233203003030003122302330111105200
010 333033303320032030313310302302000200310201000220021
010 30310321033030200030023003301110952301
011 321032213221021020103220201021200110011111101111111
011 20202110010011111111111111132111110521
012 33313320332103203020323130333031111003203130012201
012 303003100333130301121032003301111052101
013 333032313220031031303130302331100120021031200122013
013 3230023003303030011001100130111109521
014 120122110221120210201102301330110310031001200112011
014 10200230021110100021101111123102105210
015 222122212220021021313010201131200331010031300122001
015 20300211023010200121013001101110952301
016 13103212320010130003110301332110311011032100131010
016 30201210033120110021111101221102115230
017 220122103202120121112312311010120013101111030203101
017 2130211332011021013013201312111105220
019 2330232023312313302121203011202112301210303010210011
019 20301311200302010203210122011110520
020 3200120133101100201021020010011003010100313001010131
020 102332000230121000021110012111205210
021 2221332033210311212032202022103001211301313002330030
021 3130021303002021213103101321111052101
022 2320322112310320212131102011212002110211213000110031
022 203013110200202210221110111011110520
023 3321312213331010030013000211121210031021032103133230
023 1030101032000031112120102131112095210
024 332023202230032030103230302030300010023030200011002
024 3020031103002020001102200320111105230
025 121122212231121131211121111212211111112122101111211
025 01302101121201110111201012111121052101
026 2220232013201330111121201121201011011103110011101310
026 20311230122021311121222123121111052101
027 2331223032301302302112221123102122102110122011122210
027 01211301310010113211211021121121052201
028 2331222112201210201122212021202101211211112001221121
028 21211021121120101121122023211121052011
```

Figure 1.1. Data set: pre- and post-performance scores for 28 students.

THE BENEFITS OF USING STATISTICAL PROCEDURES

Essentially there are three benefits of using statistical procedures. These are the focus of this book.

1. *To summarize information and present it in a straightforward, compelling manner.* Some statistics called "measures of central tendency" allow *one* number to indicate the central message of a group of scores. A singular number can tell us how our students performed in the set of test data in figure 1.1. This is of great value to educational leaders. The measures (means, medians, and modes) are used often to make decisions. Another type of statistic is used to qualify the message of central tendency. It is called "variability," and it can show how much dispersion or spread there is in your data set of scores. Again, from a single number we can tell if a group of students is performing similarly or disparately to a group in the same grade level across other schools in the district, region, or state, and even across the nation. Without these two types of statistics, the performance test scores in figure 1.1 cannot tell us much. They only have value when statistical techniques are applied to them.
2. *To tell us whether something we did had an impact and was worthwhile, so that we can take action.* Statistics can be used to provide empirical evidence on which we can make sound decisions. Statistical procedures can tell us how seriously we should regard differences among sets of student scores. Did gains in performance occur by chance, or are they statistically significant? What instructional technique works best with a given group of students (such as those in special education)? Did the new program make a difference? What impact did our policy have? Should we maintain the status quo or make a change? Should this program be modified, and, if so, in what way? Educational leaders can make smart choices with just a few simple statistical techniques, such as *t*-tests, one-way analysis of variance procedures, and chi square analyses. These are discussed in this primer.
3. *To document relationships that are meaningful so that we can take action.* Correlation statistics can tell us whether two events are re-

lated, and to what degree. Similar to the previously stated purpose, we can use these data to make decisions and to take action. For example, what is the relationship between college-bound seniors' grade-point averages and their SAT performance? Do students who are absent from school get suspended more often? Is having breakfast related to reading readiness? Is parent involvement related to logistical support (child care, transportation)? What impact does our secondary school program have on subsequent college preparedness?

For educational leaders who want to make data-driven decisions, statistical procedures are the fundamental tools. Today, data are relied on more often and from more stakeholders of public education to obtain answers. To correctly provide those answers, educational leaders must be comfortable in determining what data are needed and then collecting, ordering, sorting, categorizing, summarizing, manipulating, and reporting what data are compiled. Statistics can make the process smooth and ultimately make life easy for the most critical step—interpreting what you find out. This will be the basis for smart decisions and action steps in your school settings.

TWO TYPES OF DATA: QUANTITATIVE AND QUALITATIVE

Using statistics involves collecting information called data, analyzing it, and making meaningful decisions based on the data. Collected data, which represent observations or measurements of something of interest, can be classified into two general types: qualitative and quantitative.

- The term *qualitative data* refers to observations that are descriptive. These data represent categories. This might include demographic data, including gender, ethnicity, marital status, religion, school location (rural, urban, and suburban), occupation, and school type (elementary, middle, and secondary).
- The term *quantitative data* represents various observations or measurements that are numeric, such as weight, height, standardized

test performance, number of students eating subsidized lunches, school attendance rates, academic achievement, library usage, enrollment data, stakeholder satisfaction, and SAT performance.

THE KEY INGREDIENT IN DATA: VARIABLES

Data are derived from characteristics about individuals, objects, or events. These characteristics are called *variables*. Anything that varies and can be measured is called a variable. Variables can be quantitative or qualitative. We attach numbers to our variables in an effort to measure them and apply statistics to them.

Class rank, SAT score, age, ethnicity, school attendance, college placement, teacher satisfaction, parental support, student suspensions, household composition, homework completion, school climate, program enrollment (special education, gifted/talented), school image, bullying, student attitudes, math achievement, bus transportation, budgets, and personnel are examples of the many variables we can measure in education.

Variables that are qualitative are called *categorical* variables. They have different categories, and each category takes on a whole number or integer to represent it. For example, school type would be a categorical variable. For some school systems it might have three categories:

1 = Elementary
2 = Middle
3 = Secondary

The variable of gender has two categories: males and females. Males can be assigned a "1" and females, a "2," or vice versa.

Variables that are quantitative are classified as either *discrete* or *continuous*. If they are discrete, they can take on only whole numbers or integers. For example, discrete variables might include household size, classroom size, total numbers of special education students, SAT scores, annual suspensions, or faculty absences. These are represented by whole numbers. If they are continuous variables, they can take on fractions or decimals. Grade reporting, chronological age, reading

Qualitive Data	Categorical variables	Whole numbers only	Types of schools: Elementary (1) Middle (2) Secondary (3)
Quantitative Data	Discrete variables	Whole numbers only	Class size 30, 25, 15
	Continuous variables	Fractions and decimals	Grade Point Average 3.29 2.33

Figure 1.2.   Classification chart for data and variables.

level, and weight are examples of continuous variables. Grade-point average, for example, might be 3.27.

A chart is presented in figure 1.2 to simplify the classification of variables.

All educational variables are measurable, or they would not be called variables. We have to assign numbers to all of our variables to apply statistics to them. To do this we have to understand the scales of measurement. This is essential. Unfortunately, it is an area that is largely misunderstood. If measurement scales are used incorrectly, the wrong statistical technique will be applied to the data and will yield erroneous information. If a decision or action step is built on poor information, it creates a problem that could be expensive, embarrassing, and even detrimental to the health and well-being of your school system and your stakeholders—especially students.

GIVING VARIABLES A NUMBER: FOUR MEASUREMENT SCALES

Whatever exists does so in some amount and can be measured. *Measurement* involves quantifying people, objects, or events on their characteristics. When we collect information about people, objects, and events, we must turn that information into numbers so that we can measure it and make deductions about what we find out. We must express it in numbers, not just descriptive phrases.

We cannot claim that our school system has a good organizational climate, or high performance on standardized tests, or declining absenteeism, or increased faculty development, or excellent college placement rates unless we measure or apply numbers to these perceptions. We have to give "teeth," or substance, to these allegations. Data can do the job for us.

Because measurement entails quantifying people, objects, or events on their characteristics, you must assign numbers to variables. There are four scales of measurement used to assign numbers to variables. They are differentiated according to their degree of *precision*. For example, a physical education teacher might measure a child's physical fitness by the child's performance on specific exercises *and* by degree of body fat. The second factor is a more precise measure, although both can provide information about the same variable—of physical fitness.

There are four measurement scales that are used often in educational settings: nominal, ordinal, interval, and ratio.

Nominal Measurement Scales

The first measurement scale in the hierarchy is the nominal scale. The root of the term *nominal* means to name. The properties of nominal scales are that

- Data categories are mutually exclusive.
- Data categories have no logical order.

Observations are simply classified into categories and assigned a number with no relationship existing between or among the categories. This scale classifies without ordering. The variable gender can be nominally scaled with a number of either 1 or 2 assigned to male or female categories. Another example is the variable of school location; it would have nominal scaling. The numeric values could be any combination. Three possibilities are presented in figure 1.3.

Option 1		Option 2		Option 3	
Variable	Numbers Assigned	Variable	Numbers Assigned	Variable	Numbers Assigned
Rural	1	Rural	2	Rural	3
Urban	2	Urban	3	Urban	1
Suburban	3	Suburban	1	Suburban	2

Figure 1.3. Three nominal scale options for the variable of school location.

There is no logical ordering of the categories. Numbers are assigned to the categories, but no quantitative meaning is assigned to the numbers. The numbers mean absolutely *nothing*. We are simply using the numbers to classify people, objects, and events. The numbers we assign to those categories have no ordering, no ranking, no "higher than," no "lower than," no "more of," or no "less than" associated with them. They are what their name suggests—nominal, a name to identify. The numbers we assign to our variables in their categories are not quantifiable except to count them. How many males we have will be how many we add up with the value we have assigned to this category of either 1 or 2. This is important to note when you are calculating statistics.

There are two basic requirements for nominal measurement:

1. All members of one category must be assigned the same numeral.
2. No two categories are assigned the same numeral.

Some nominal-scaled variables have only two categories. These are called *dichotomous* variables. This means that only two numbers can be assigned to each of the categories, respectively. Some examples of dichotomous variables include gender (male and female), language (English/ Spanish), parent (father/mother), staff (administrator/teacher), student (special education/regular education), college placement (accepted/rejected), and voter (registered/not registered). You may use two numbers (such as 1 and 2 *or* 0 and 1 *or* 200 and 300) as the nominal scaling applied to each category.

Nominal scaling is ideal to categorize the schools in a school system in order to disaggregate data sets. *Type of school* the child attends might be categorized as elementary (1), middle (2), and secondary (3). Or, if there are five elementary schools, we could nominally scale all of the schools that the children in a town attend as shown in figure 1.4.

Being able to nominally scale our variables this way allows us to inspect our data much more intimately. Think about how much information you would miss if you had to consolidate all the schools together instead of

Schools in the School System	Number Assigned
Torringford Elementary School	1
Southwest Elementary School	2
Forbes Elementary School	3
East Elementary School	4
Vogel Wetmore Elementary School	5
Torrington Middle School	6
Torrington High School	7

Figure 1.4. Nominal scale for a seven-school system with three elementary schools.

separating them by individual categories. With nominal scaling you *can isolate by school (category)* the following information:

- What does student performance look like by classroom, grade level, or school?
- How many new students does each school have at the beginning of the school year?
- How is the ethnicity of the students broken down by school?
- How many students require subsidized lunches by school?
- How many are using bus transportation by school?
- Are there differences among schools in referrals to special education?
- How many ELL (English Language Learners) students are there per school?
- Which school has the most suspensions?

One huge pitfall looms. Many individuals get confused about what the actual variable is and what are the respective categories. Sometimes, educators think the variable is female or male instead of gender with two categories. This differentiation is very important especially when you are investigating statistical differences with inferential statistics, which will be discussed in chapter 6. Ask yourself: What variable is being represented by the individual categories? The answer should be the variable itself and not its categories.

Ordinal Measurement Scales

The second type of scaling in the measurement hierarchy is called *ordinal,* in which there is relative ranking and ordering of an attribute in different categories. There is "more than" and "less than," "higher than" and "lower than," and "least of" and "most of." There is a qualitative relationship among numbers in the ordinal scale. Unlike nominal scaling, the numbers in ordinal scales have meaning. Ordinal scales give more information and more precise data than nominal scales do. Here are three examples of ordinal-scaled variables:

Variable: Frequency

Never (0)	Rarely (1)	Sometimes (2)	Frequently (3)	Always (4)

Variable: Satisfaction

Dissatisfied (1)	Satisfied (2)	Very Satisfied (3)

Variable: Performance Assessment Attainment

Goal Not Attained (1)	Goal Attained (2)	Goal Exceeded (3)

The properties of ordinal scales are that

- Data categories are mutually exclusive.
- Data categories have some logical order.
- Data categories are scaled according to the amount of a particular characteristic they possess.

One of the most common uses of ordinal scaling is with ratings, preferences, rankings, goal attainment, satisfaction, degrees of quality, and agreement levels—typical of the Likert scales on questionnaires. When you are asked to rate something and are given several choices, the scales used are ordinal. The response categories are ordered with numbers assigned to them that reflect the order of the response. Here is an example of responses assigned with ordinal scaling.

Responses on a Questionnaire Using Ordinal Scales	Numbers Assigned
Poor	1

Fair	2
Good	3
Very Good	4
Excellent	5

It is helpful to assign your numbers in ordinal scaling in ways that make sense. A rating of "excellent" can have a value of 5 or a value of 1. It is relatively arbitrary. However, it makes more conceptual sense that a value of 1 should be assigned to a low rating, such as "poor," whereas a high number (5) should be assigned to a high rating, such as "excellent." After you tabulate your data, it is easier to interpret what you have found out if you assign your ordinal numbers in gradations that make sense.

Another example of ordinal scaling that is used often in education is applied to agreement statements. There are four responses that could be assigned ordinal values. Again, it makes more conceptual sense to assign the value "1" to the least amount of agreement— "Strongly Disagree"—and vice versa. Higher levels of agreement should be reflected in the values assigned, such as 4 = "Strongly Agree." Again, this is arbitrary.

Agreement Scale on a Questionnaire	Numbers Assigned
Strongly Disagree	1
Disagree	2
Agree	3
Strongly Agree	4

As a note, several educational studies use "No Opinion" as a fifth response on agreement statements. This practice is not recommended, because everyone has an opinion. A "no opinion" response provides a loophole that creates missing data. However, if you do use it, the value assigned should be a zero (0). It has been used in education studies as a middle response and assigned a value of "3." This is incorrect. No opinion is no opinion and should be reflected with a numeric value that makes sense—a zero. It should not be given a numeric rating that will confound the statistics that you obtain by its misrepresentation.

Interval and Ratio Measurement Scales

There are two metric scales of measurement. They are called *interval* and *ratio* scales. Because of their metric nature, these two measurement scales afford the most precise data. With both there are equal intervals or units between any two consecutive numbers. The only difference between interval and ratio scales is the role of zero. In interval scales, zero is artificial rather than real. Intelligence quotient (IQ) and standardized tests for performance assessment have a zero, but it is artificially created rather than real. In ratio scales, zero is real. It signifies the absence of the variable under study. Ratio scales are used often in the biological and physical sciences for variables such as weight, height, calories, and so forth. Interval scales are used more often in disciplines such as education.

All standardized testing, the SAT and ACT, achievement tests, mastery tests, IQ tests, some vocational tests, and many other assessment tools rely on the metric-based measurement scales. When data compiled from attendance rates, dropout rates, graduation rates, suspension rates, and special education referral rates are used, for example, the data are reported using these measurement scales.

Because it is possible to assign real numbers to variables, we can compare our data with other sets of data from similar classrooms, schools, school systems, states, regions, the nation, and even other countries. With these two scales we can compute high-level, sophisticated statistics called parametric statistics (which will be discussed in chapter 6).

The properties of interval scales include the following:

- Data categories are mutually exclusive.
- Data categories have a definite logical order.
- Data categories are scaled according to the amount of a particular characteristic they possess.
- Equal differences in the characteristics are represented by equal differences in the numbers assigned to the categories.
- The zero (0) point is just another point on the scale.

For interval scales, the distances between the numbers 2 and 3 and between 4 and 5 are exactly the same. This is different from ordinal scales, where we cannot claim for certain that the distance between good (3) and fair (2) is exactly the same as between poor (1) and fair (2). We assign numbers in ordinal scales, but the distance is not in exact intervals. With interval scales, there is the ordering that is found in ordinal scales but now we have exact units of measurement.

Interval scales have a zero (0) point in them, but it is arbitrary. Good examples are the interval scales used for temperature: Fahrenheit and Celsius. The difference between 15° Celsius and 20° Celsius is 5°. The same is true for Fahrenheit. But there is no absence of temperature. The zero is an arbitrary point in both scales. The same is true for IQ scales. There is an arbitrary zero, but there is no absence of intelligence in human beings (although sometimes it may appear so).

Ratio scaling is similar to interval scaling in terms of equivalent values between numbers. The only difference is that in ratio scales a zero (0) means something important. It means the absence of whatever the scale is measuring. This type of scaling is encountered more commonly in the physical sciences, where there can really be "no" weight, time, height, or water pressure, or wherever zero is real and not artificially created.

The properties of ratio scales are as follows:

- Data categories are mutually exclusive.
- Data categories have a definite logical order.
- Data categories are scaled according to the amount of a particular characteristic they possess.
- Equal differences in the characteristics are represented by equal differences in the numbers assigned to the categories.
- The zero (0) point reflects absence of the characteristic.

CONCLUSION

The four measurement scales can be remembered by the following characteristics:

- *Nominal:* numbers are assigned without order.
- *Ordinal:* numbers are assigned with order but without equal intervals between them.
- *Interval:* numbers are assigned with order and equal units.
- *Ratio:* numbers are assigned with order, equal units, and a true zero point.

When educational leaders are setting up their data warehouses, it is essential to know the information covered in this first chapter. Knowing what the differences in measurement scales are, selecting the correct measurement scales for variables, and identifying which ones you use for different statistical procedures are absolutely the most significant steps in setting up data warehouses for data-driven decisions. This understanding is vital; the use of statistical procedures depends on this basic knowledge. If you apply the wrong scale of measurement to a statistical procedure, the result could be a data-driven decision based on faulty information. This can be expensive, distressing, and wasteful—not to mention detrimental.

❷

EVERY PICTURE TELLS A STORY

Most of the time when we look at a set of data there is not much that we can conclude from it. It is basically a blur of numbers. This is easily overcome by displaying data with a "method to the madness." There are several steps that educational leaders should follow when they are working with data sets. The first step is simply organizing the data because an unordered set of scores is not convenient to work with. Many individuals skip this step because it is elementary and seems too simplistic to be useful. Take the time to organize your data. Doing this will help you both to understand the data and to make preliminary conclusions. Equally important, you will become familiar with the data to the point where no embarrassing oversights can be pointed to later on at a board of education meeting or by the local media.

FREQUENCY DISTRIBUTIONS

When a set of data is presented to you, one of the most useful expenditures of time is to construct a *frequency distribution*. A frequency distribution is a systematic arrangement of numeric values from the highest to the lowest—together with a count of the number of times each value was obtained. It is a procedure for organizing and summarizing data into a meaningful representation. It does not tell you everything about your information, but it provides a beginning, a convenient way of grouping data so that meaningful patterns can be found.

The first step in developing a frequency distribution is to put all of the scores in order from the lowest value to the highest value. Put them in a column format. Then, use slash marks or tally marks beside every score in your column—each and every time it occurs. Some scores may occur only once, and some may occur more often. This is why tally marks are helpful. Lastly, count up the tally marks and place a real number beside them that shows the frequency with which each value occurred in your distribution. This information in a chart form can make sense of a set of numbers that appears to be a jumble at first glance.

There are symbols that are typically used. When we set up our frequency distributions, the lowercase letter x indicates our scores and the lowercase letter f indicates the frequency of occurrence.

HOW TO CONSTRUCT A FREQUENCY DISTRIBUTION

The data in figure 2.1 are SAT math scores for a special group of students who were selected to participate in a high school math enrichment program. The lowest SAT math score is 320, and the highest is 699. The frequency distribution shown in figure 2.2 orders the 50 scores from lowest to highest, and then tally marks are placed to show the frequency with which each score was obtained. Percentages (the relative frequencies) are calculated to provide even more information. Finally, cumulative frequencies and cumulative percentages are added to complete the picture.

From this frequency distribution, you can draw some important conclusions.

- Most of the scores were low.
- The most frequently occurring score was 420.
- There is a broad range of scores from highest (699) to lowest (320).
- Ninety-six percent of the students got a score below 500.
- Two scores (699 and 689) were very different from other scores.
- More than half of the students scored 430 or below.

699	459	450	450	445
420	420	420	420	420
430	420	445	435	467
420	320	420	320	420
689	445	479	450	467
435	430	430	430	420
420	467	467	450	435
320	320	320	320	420
430	445	430	435	467
420	420	320	420	420

Figure 2.1. Data set of SAT math scores for fifty students.

(N = 50)

SATM	Tallies	Frequency (f)	Relative Frequency (%)	Cumulative Frequency	Cumulative Frequency (%)
320	///////	7	14%	7	14%
420	///////////////	15	30%	22	44%
430	//////	6	12%	28	56%
435	////	4	8%	32	64%
445	////	4	8%	36	72%
450	////	4	8%	40	80%
459	/	1	2%	41	82%
467	//////	6	12%	47	94%
479	/	1	2%	48	96%
689	/	1	2%	49	98%
699	/	1	2%	50	100%

Figure 2.2.   Frequency distribution of SAT math scores.

Class Intervals

Sometimes your data set is not as simple as the SAT data set in terms of the number of student scores and the values of the student data. Let's say that you have a large sample of student data—100 verbal scores on the SAT.

You might want to use a "shorthand" called *class intervals*. The number of classifications of data (classes) can be reduced by combining several of the actual scores into an interval or band of scores. You are essentially consolidating the data into bundles to make it more manageable and comprehensible.

A good rule of thumb is to have between 10 and 20 class intervals. This is particularly true if you intend to graph your frequency distribution data into a frequency polygon or histogram, which will be discussed shortly. Ten to 20 class intervals will summarize your data without distorting the shape of your graph. Too few intervals compress the data and thus conceal meaningful changes in the shape that you graph. Too many intervals stretch out the data and so they are not summarized enough for a clear visualization.

There are two general rules for using class intervals:

1. The class interval should be of such size that between 10 and 20 intervals will cover the total range of scores. This provides for a manageable number of intervals without losing the general shape of the distribution of scores.
2. Whenever possible, the width of the class interval should be an odd rather than an even number. Under this rule, the midpoint of the interval will be a whole number rather than a fraction. This will become important when you graph your data.

How to Construct a Frequency Distribution Using Class Intervals

- First, determine the range in your frequency distribution from your highest score to your lowest. For the point of illustration, we have a low score of 320 and a high score of 767. The difference, or *range,* is (767 minus 320) 447.
- Divide the range by either 10 or 20 to get the number of intervals that makes the most sense and is most manageable for you. For 10, you would divide 447 by 10 and it would yield 45 as the class interval. For 20, you would divide 447 by 20 and get 22 as the class interval. For the sake of illustration we choose 10, so our class interval is 45.

- Begin your intervals a little below your lowest score, which in our data is 320. So let's start with 254–299 as our first interval. With 45 increments, our next class interval is 300–344.
- Once you set up your class intervals, then you proceed the same way you did with the frequency distribution in figure 2.2. Use tallies for the interval in which your student's score falls. A tally would note a score of 396 in the interval of 391–436.

Figure 2.3 displays what our frequency distribution with class intervals would look like.

As you can see, using class intervals to compose a frequency distribution makes it easy to analyze as well as to present your data. Again, important conclusions can be drawn.

- Most of the scores were low.
- The most frequently occurring scores were between 391 and 436.
- There is a broad range of scores, from below 345 to over 758.
- Fifty percent of the students got a score below 483.
- There were a few extremely high and extremely low scores.

Class Intervals of 45	Tallies	Frequency (f)	Relative Frequency (%)	Cumulative Frequency	Cumulative Frequency (%)
254–299					
300–344	/	1	1%	1	1%
345–390	//////	6	6%	7	7%
391–436	/////////////////////////	25	25%	32	32%
437–482	//////////////////	18	18%	50	50%
483–528	///////////	11	11%	61	61%
529–574	////////////	12	12%	73	73%
575–620	/////////	9	9%	82	82%
621–666	//////	6	6%	88	88%
667–712	//////	6	6%	94	94%
713–758	/////	5	5%	99	99%
759–800	/	1	1%	100	100%

Figure 2.3. Frequency distribution of SAT verbal scores with class intervals.

As a note, using class intervals is less cumbersome when your data are continuous and have a wide range of values. Think about the variable of *age* and the adult population in your community if you were conducting a community survey. To list all possible ages of adults could start at 18 and go beyond 100 or more years! Doing a tally of each and every age would require a lot of paper, never mind time. This is a case when categorizing your variable into class intervals is a good idea. You might use intervals of five years in this case so that there would be fewer than 20 intervals for adult ages, and those class intervals would look like this.

Class Intervals for Age
18–22
23–27
28–32
33–37
38–42
43–47
48–52
53–57
58–62
63–67
68–72 and so forth.

On the other hand, there are times when using class intervals short-changes the picture: you lose valuable data. Think about the variable *"years that teachers have been in the field of education."* If you used class intervals, you would lose key information. A teacher who is brand new, one who has been with you for only one year, and one who has been on staff for two years may be very different from each other. If you collapsed the "years" in the field of education into intervals of five as just shown, you would lose important insights. Much of this is common sense. Think out what value the information has to you for data-driven decisions. What is the information you want to uncover with your data?

WHY FREQUENCY DISTRIBUTIONS ARE HELPFUL

Whenever you compile a set of data for a data-driven decision it is highly recommended that you first set up a frequency distribution and study it.

Knowing your data intimately is critical before you begin to delve deeper into knowing what it means. Besides developing an expertise with your data set, there are several practical aspects to the development of frequency distributions.

- You can identify atypical or odd scores like those in figure 2.2 (SAT math 699 and 689). What should you do with those types of scores? How should you treat data that are not representative of the group?
- You can tell how spread out the scores of different groups are. If you set up two frequency distributions representing two third-grade classrooms and their performance on achievement tests, you may see that the scores are similar. Should you combine the groups and have a larger sample size?
- Seeing the frequency with which each value occurred in the distribution could help you to make decisions about statistical analyses you will execute later on. This is particularly true with categorical variables. For example, if ethnicity shows few members in one category, you may want to combine it with another that is similar to it so that statistical analyses can be executed.
- Finally, the frequency distribution may reveal data entry errors that you typed in accidentally. If you had a value of 899 on the SAT math data, you would know that that was an incorrect entry. You would be able to make your correction and not run the data blindly, thus compromising the purity of your data set.

GRAPHING

The frequency distribution is an excellent tool for displaying data and inspecting your data. Yet, tables, as comprehensive as they are, do not convey the information as quickly or as impressively as graphs do. Graphing allows us to see the shape of a distribution. They are designed to help the user obtain an intuitive feeling for the data at a glance. The message of the data should be readily apparent and the story obvious.

An effective graph is simple and clean. It should not attempt to present so much information that it is difficult to comprehend. It should be complete within itself and require little explanation in the narrative.

Benefits of Using Graphs

Graphs are most beneficial to educational leaders because they can provide a summary data sheet as well as an opportunity to visualize your data. By looking at the *shape of the curve* in your graph you can make some general conclusions fairly quickly about the scores in your data set. The illustrations in figure 2.4 will help in interpreting shapes.

- If the curve has a hump in the middle, its symmetry means that you have most scores in the middle of the range—few high and few low scores. (A)
- If the hump of the curve is toward the left, you have more low scores in your data set. The tail of this type of curve indicates atypical or high scores in your data set. (B)
- If the hump of the curve is toward the right, you have more high scores in your data set. The tail of this type of curve indicates atypical or low scores in your data set. (C)
- If the hump of the curve is flat, you have scores that are spread out a great deal. Scores are "all over the map." (D)
- If the hump of the curve is peaked, your scores are very, very similar. There is not much difference among scores. (E)
- If there are two or even three humps in the graph, you have overlapping groups whose scores are different from each other. (F)

The discussion about shapes of graphs will have more meaning after you read chapters 3 and 4.

Frequency Polygons

To construct a graph from a set of data, we start with the frequency distribution. A frequency distribution can be graphed into a *frequency polygon.* This is how you convert a frequency distribution into a frequency polygon.

Draw a vertical side, or *ordinate,* axis of your graph. This is called the *y*-axis. On the *y*-axis it is an accepted practice for the frequencies to be plotted. The horizontal axis, called the *abscissa,* is used to plot the variable that you are displaying data for. The horizontal axis is the *x*-axis. As a rule of thumb for good visual presentation, the vertical axis should be roughly two-thirds the length of the horizontal axis.

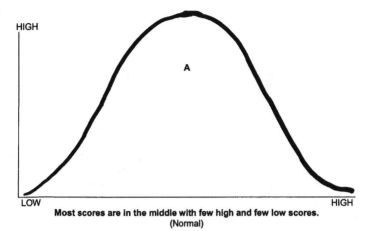

Most scores are in the middle with few high and few low scores.
(Normal)

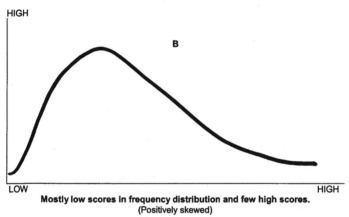

Mostly low scores in frequency distribution and few high scores.
(Positively skewed)

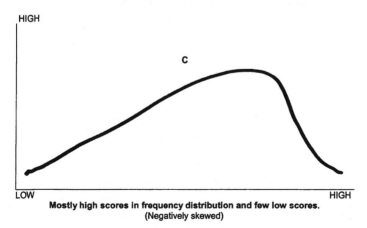

Mostly high scores in frequency distribution and few low scores.
(Negatively skewed)

Figure 2.4. Interpreting the shapes of curves in frequency polygons (A to F).

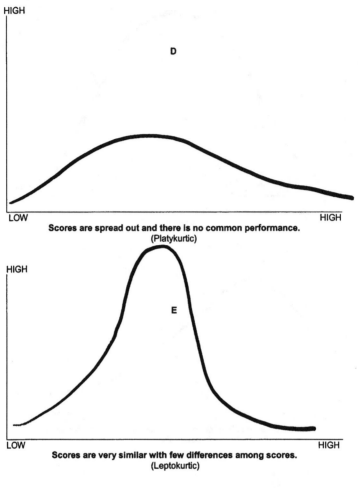

Scores are spread out and there is no common performance.
(Platykurtic)

Scores are very similar with few differences among scores.
(Leptokurtic)

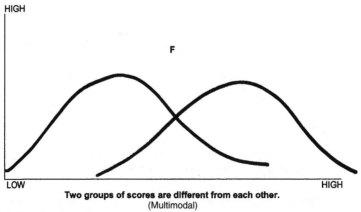

Two groups of scores are different from each other.
(Multimodal)

Figure 2.4. **Continued.**

Connect the points or dots that intersect from the scores or score interval on the abscissa to the frequencies noted on the ordinate axes. If class intervals are used, connect the midpoint of the interval on the horizontal axis with the frequency on the vertical axis. This is why it is helpful to use odd numbers for the span of your class interval. The midpoint is easy to identify.

As a note, if the range in frequencies is large, you may want to start the vertical axis with a value that is not zero (0). When you do this, it is a good idea to use a jagged edge in the beginning of your vertical line so that it is clear that there is a break in the scale. With our SAT data we do not need this because we are starting at the low end of the SAT distribution of scores. The SAT range actually begins with the score of 200.

A frequency polygon for our verbal SAT data with class intervals looks like that depicted in figure 2.5.

Plotting the data this way allows the graph to take on a shape. When you look at that shape, you can make a conclusion about the data from the frequency distribution. When there are a lot of data from many subjects, the frequency polygon looks like a smooth curve. When there are fewer values, it is jagged. Either way, the picture tells a story. This is a picture that gives us an immediate message about our data. We look at it and we can infer something about our data. For our SAT graphs, the simple message is that there are many low scores in this distribution.

We can also construct a cumulative frequency polygon from our frequency distribution if we have included cumulative data (figure 2.6).

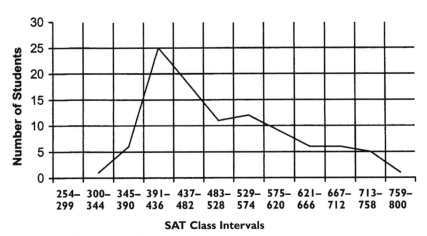

Figure 2.5.   Frequency polygon.

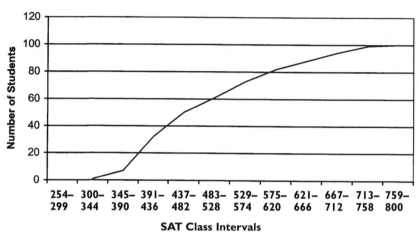

Figure 2.6. Cumulative frequency polygon.

We can either use the cumulative frequencies or use the percentages on the vertical axis, where 100% is the highest value and 0% is the lowest value. Cumulative frequency polygons are known as *ogives*.

Histograms, Bar Graphs, and Pictographs

A *histogram* is another pictorial representation of a frequency distribution table. The vertical scale should begin at zero (0). Again, use the jagged edge if you cannot begin it with zero. A general rule in laying out the histogram is to make the height of the vertical scale equal to approximately two-thirds the length of the horizontal scale. Otherwise, the histogram may appear to be out of proportion.

A vertical bar is constructed above each class interval equal in height to its frequency. All of the rectangles have equal width. This is a very common way to display data. You can also set up a cumulative frequency histogram, as we did with cumulative frequency polygons. We can use the cumulative frequencies or we can use the percentages on the vertical axis, where 100% is the highest value and 0% is the lowest value. Figure 2.7 displays what a histogram would look like for our SAT data with class intervals.

A *bar graph* (also called a *bar chart*) is a very convenient graphing device that is particularly useful for displaying nominal data such as gender and ethnicity. The various categories are located along the horizontal axis. The frequency, as always, is on the vertical axis. The height of

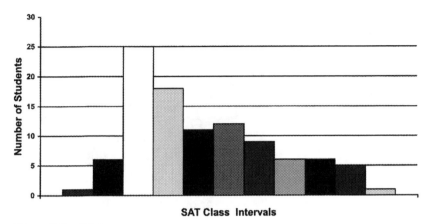

SAT Class Intervals

Figure 2.7. Histogram.

each bar is equal to the frequency for that category. This is very helpful to see differences in your data for individual groups on some variable.

One difference between a histogram and a bar graph is that with the histogram the bars are placed next to each other to show when one interval begins and the other one ends. The data are continuous, and are interval/ratio scaled. However, because the data are nominal in bar graphs, we do not connect the bars, preventing any implication of continuity. We separate the bars and use equal space to separate one bar from the next. Drawing the bars in a bar graph creates ease in interpretation. A bar graph of middle schools and their respective special education referral rates is displayed in figure 2.8.

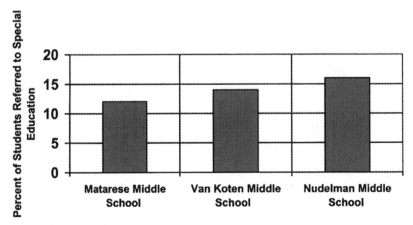

Figure 2.8. Bar graph.

Number of Children

	1	2	3	4	5	6	7	8	9	10	11
7				📖	📖	📖	📖	📖			
6				📖	📖	📖	📖	📖			
5				📖	📖	📖	📖	📖			
4				📖	📖	📖	📖	📖			
3		📖	📖	📖	📖	📖	📖	📖	📖	📖	
2	📖	📖	📖	📖	📖	📖	📖	📖	📖	📖	📖
1	📖	📖	📖	📖	📖	📖	📖	📖	📖	📖	📖
0	1	2	3	4	5	6	7	8	9	10	11

Number of Books Read

Figure 2.9.   Pictograph.

A simplified version of the bar graph is the *pictograph*, which uses columns of pictures or symbols in place of bars. Figure 2.9 portrays a pictograph of the number of books read by a number of students.

Pie Charts

Another method to display categorical data is by using a *pie chart*. It is very easy and user-friendly. You can show categories of a variable by dividing up "the pie." Use 100% of the area in the circle and divide it up proportionally to your categories of interest. Figure 2.10 displays a pie chart that reflects a secondary school faculty and the types of degrees the faculty members hold.

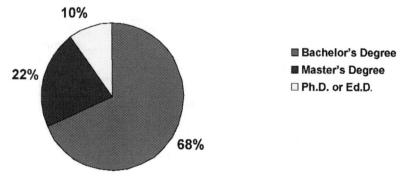

Figure 2.10.   Pie chart.

Constructing Your Graphs

Graphs are an excellent way to demonstrate your data to the un-trained eye. Take advantage of their ability to tell your story. There are two recommendations to observe when constructing your graphs.

1. A graph is a picture, so the message should be readily apparent. KISS (Keep it simple, stupid) is a good rule to follow when graph-ing or even when constructing your tables. Remember, those who will be viewing the graph or reading your reports are not as in-volved in your data and analysis as you are and have other thoughts competing for their attention. Do not waste their time with graphs that are either overly simplistic or overly complex. Use graphs ju-diciously and with thoughtful deliberation.

2. Avoid the temptation to emphasize your point or position by "adjust-ing" the vertical axis. This creates a *truncated* graph. The vertical scale is cut off or restricted so that the information becomes distorted. The picture is misleading. This is a common practice that the media often use in reporting or sensationalizing stories for the public (who may have an untrained eye). The axes are exaggerated so that the graph presents dramatic results that really were rather " ho hum." Good ex-amples of graphs that mislead people are often presented in the news media when standardized or mastery test performance data are shown. The vertical axis is restricted to a short range, causing overem-phasis of the results in either a positive or negative light. The graph in figure 2.11 reports a "steep decline in SAT scores." But look how the vertical scale has been adjusted to begin at 485, distorting the picture. The drop over a three-year period is negligible—from 502 to 496! A glance at the graph would cause your secondary school principal to faint before he or she could find out the real story from the data.

CONCLUSION

The process of becoming an expert with your data is tough work. Setting up the frequency distribution for your data set, graphing it, and then in-terpreting what it conveys are often-skipped steps in data management.

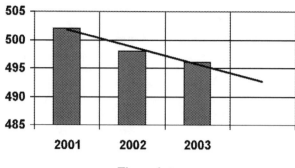

The real story...

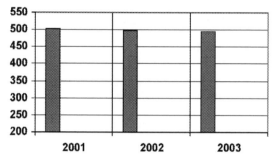

Figure 2.11. The "steep" decline in SAT scores over three years.

This is unfortunate. The time it takes to do the grunt work as a preliminary step is a worthwhile investment of time. There are advantages to be gained in many areas. You will be able to reduce errors, make wise decisions about statistical techniques, and ultimately provide a better foundation for your data-driven decisions. This has implications that are far-reaching. Take the time to get intimate with your data set. The value will be well worth the hours spent.

❸

DON'T BE SEDUCED BY THE MEAN

The process of simplifying your data set to get to know it was presented in chapter 2. The frequency distribution and the graphs that portray these data are methods of describing your data set. There are also certain statistics that are generated for the purpose of describing the distributions of your data or the relationships between your variables. They are called *descriptive statistics*. These very useful statistics bring together large amounts of data so they can be presented and comprehended with minimal effort.

Descriptive statistics are widely applied. A good example of a real-life application is the U.S. Census. By using some of the popular descriptive statistics, we get a sense of important characteristics of households in the United States. For example, descriptive statistics that are available in U.S. Census data may indicate:

- Average household size
- Ethnic and gender breakdowns
- Employment rates
- Average cost of single family homes and rental units
- Percent of children in different age categories
- Per capita income
- High school completion rates

Schools can do the same thing with important variables such as class size, standardized test scores, school attendance rates, ethnic breakdown, birth rates, college placement, and dropout rates, to name just a few. If we had to generate this type of information from looking at raw data, it would be too complex to grasp and to readily understand. Descriptive statistics make it easy to get a sense of what is typical or average.

Measures of *central tendency* represent an important collection of descriptive statistics. These are designed to describe the *central part* of the distribution that you created with your frequency distribution. They tell where most scores appear to group, cluster, or fall together—their commonality. In other words, they tell us the average. With one single number you can obtain an accurate picture of your entire distribution. It suggests the typical performance of a group as a whole and is a concise description.

There are three measures of central tendency: the mean, the median, and the mode.

THE MEAN

The *mean* represents a whole data set of scores with one single number! The mean is the arithmetic average value in your distribution of scores. To obtain the mean you add up all of the scores (x) and divide by the total number of scores in your distribution. As a rule, your data set of scores should tend to cluster together and not be spread all over. The beauty of the mean is that you utilize each and every score in your distribution to calculate it. As a result, it is the most stable measure of central tendency and the one used most often. Because it is an average, you probably have been calculating a mean often in your everyday life.

Here is a simple example to illustrate the use of the mean. During this past school year, the board of education was contemplating the creation of additional elementary school classroom space. Three neighborhood elementary schools were brimming with children. This was primarily because of families moving from cities to a suburban location. So the board members decided to find out what the average class size was to arm themselves with supporting data for overcrowding and ultimately to argue for additional classroom space.

Although class sizes were compiled for all grade levels, the data set for 10 second grade classrooms was reported as shown in figure 3.1.

Second Grade Classrooms	Class Size
Class 1	28
Class 2	28
Class 3	29
Class 4	29
Class 5	29
Class 6	31
Class 7	31
Class 8	32
Class 9	32
Class 10	33
Mean	**30**

Figure 3.1. Class-size data for second grade classrooms.

The mean was calculated as 30 students per classroom. Here was the evidence the board of education needed. With just one number representing all 10 schools the board had a solid piece of information for data-driven decisions.

The mean is a very good measure of central tendency:

- It is based on more precise measurement scales such as interval and ratio. Sometimes ordinal data are used, too. This may occur with rating scales, performance scales, or satisfaction scales in which averages are useful. Purists would object to the use of a mean with ordinal data simply because the units of measurement are not exact. However, in many educational applications, ordinal data are used with the mean because it makes sense. That is the determinant of when to apply the mean to your data if it is ordinal scaled. If it makes sense in producing good information for strategic decisions, by all means use it. Certainly, no mean can be calculated with nominal-scaled variables.
- As mentioned earlier, *all* the scores in a data set are used to calculate the mean. This is another plus.
- Finally, many of the powerful statistical analyses rely on the mean to calculate formulas for statistical significance. So the mean has become the "queen of central tendency." But this royal designation should be avoided if your data set possesses *outliers*.

An *outlier* is an extremely high or low score in your distribution. It is an *atypical* score and does not resemble most of the other scores in your distribution. It affects the calculation of the mean and makes the mean less representative of the group. Whereas the mean is looking to create typical performance in your data set, the outlier is atypical. We had two outliers in the SAT math data set in chapter 2.

What happens is that outliers cause the mean to shift in the direction of the outlier. If the outlier is a high score, the mean is calculated higher than it should be. If it is a low score, the mean is lower than it should be to represent the whole group. Outliers cause your distribution to become distorted. This problem is particularly true if the number of scores in your distribution is small.

You can tell if you have outliers in your data set by setting up a frequency distribution and then graphing a frequency polygon. If you have an asymmetrical curve, outliers are hanging around. The SAT frequency polygons and histograms in chapter 2 suffered from the existence of outliers in the data set. The curves in the graphs were irregular as opposed to being balanced.

Going back to the example of classroom size, let's alter the data set with two particularly large second grade classrooms. The data set would look like that shown in figure 3.2.

Second Grade Classrooms	Class Size
Class 1	28
Class 2	28
Class 3	29
Class 4	29
Class 5	29
Class 6	31
Class 7	31
Class 8	32
Class 9 outlier	44
Class 10 outlier	45
Mean	**33**

Figure 3.2. Class-size data for second grade classrooms with outliers.

Here, the outlier caused the mean to shift up to 33 children per class-room. Although the presence of the outlier increases the case for additional classroom space, it is not an honest representation of average class size in your school system. Most class sizes in your data set distribution are around 29 to 30. If you used the mean as the measure of central tendency in this case, you would be presenting an exaggerated picture of need. This information might eventually surface to embarrass the board of education in the presence of hard data collected by the ever-vigilant taxpayers association and the media, both of whom may have seen the hard data from which the mean was derived.

What should you do as an educational leader? Examine your data through the grunt work of developing a frequency distribution, and then use *more than one measure* of central tendency. One of the best, when your data has outliers, is the *median*.

THE MEDIAN

When there are extreme scores or outliers in your distribution, the *median* is the preferred measure of central tendency. The median is the counting average. It is simply the midpoint in your distribution of ranked, ordered scores. The median can be used with ordinal-, interval-, and ratio-scaled data. Its use with nominal data is inappropriate.

To calculate the median, list all of the values in your distribution from the lowest to the highest and then find the *midpoint*—the place where it divides your distribution into equal halves. That is, 50% of all scores are above and 50% are below.

The Median—Odd Number of Scores in Your Distribution

If there is an odd number of scores in your distribution, the median is easy to identify. Find the midpoint in the range of high to low scores. That midpoint is the median, because half of the scores are above it and half are below it. A formula can be used to locate the position in an ordered set of data:

Median = Number of scores plus 1 divided by 2

If you had 11 scores (an odd number), the formula would be (11 + 1) ÷ 2 = 6. The median would be the sixth score in the set of data where the scores are listed in order from lowest to highest.

Here is an example in which we have an odd number (11) of scores. The midpoint is the sixth score or the exact middle of the distribution. In this distribution, the median is 29 and 29 is an actual score in the data set.

Order of Scores Lowest to Highest	1st Score	2nd Score	3rd Score	4th Score	5th Score	6th Score	7th Score	8th Score	9th Score	10th Score	11th Score
The 11 Scores	28	28	29	29	29	29	31	31	32	32	33
					50%	Mid-point	50%				

The Median—Even Number of Scores in Your Distribution

If you have an even number of scores, find the two that make the centermost point and then average them. If you have an even number of scores, the median may or may not be an actual score, depending on what the two midpoints are. If the midpoints are identical scores, then this is the median. If they need to be averaged, then the median will be an average and not an actual score in your distribution. That is why we say the median is the midpoint—a point, not a score.

Here is an example of when this is true. In figure 3.2, we had our class size data with the outlier in the group. Two classrooms had 44 and 45 children each. This outlier shifted our mean up to 33. So we decide to calculate a median.

The data set consisted of 10 scores altogether—an even number of scores. So we have to find the two midpoints and average them. The 10 scores are divided in half, with 5 scores on the left and 5 scores on the right. The median is calculated by taking two scores at the midpoint or center and calculating a mean. In this case, there is a score of 29 on the left and a score of 31 on the right.

The formula becomes

[Centerpoint 1 plus Centerpoint 2] ÷ 2 = Median

In this example, the application of the formula is [29 + 31] = 60 ÷ 2 = 30 (the median).

Order of Scores Lowest to Highest	1st Score	2nd Score	3rd Score	4th Score	5th Score	6th Score	7th Score	8th Score	9th Score	10th Score
The 10 Scores	28	28	29	29	29	31	31	32	44	45

Center points

The median and midpoint of the distribution is 30. However, note that the median is not an actual score in the set of data. As you can see, the median is not affected one bit by the outliers of 44 and 45. Although the mean was a 33, the median of 30 is more representative of the data set. This is the greatest benefit of using the median. Oddball scores in the data set do not affect it. Although the median is not calculated by using all of the scores in the distribution, as the mean is, the median plays an important role in stating the central tendency of your data set—especially if there are outlier scores.

THE MODE

The *mode* is an unsophisticated measure of central tendency. It is the most frequently occurring value in your distribution. It is a simple but rough statistic to calculate the central tendency of your data. The mode does not need to be calculated. If you look at your frequency distribution, a simple eyeball inspection of your data can tell you which score occurred most often. It is quick and can be obtained with a glance. We did that in chapter 2 with our first data set of SAT math scores. We looked at the frequency distribution in figure 2.2 and could see that the mode was 420.

The mode provides little information beyond simply identifying the score in your data set that appears with the greatest frequency. Therefore, it should only be used when you have a large data set of scores, and not just a few. A small set of scores would not have enough frequency of occurrence built in it to develop a mode. You need many scores so that you can be certain which score turned up most often.

For example, in figure 3.1 our class sizes contributed to a frequency distribution that looks like this:

Class Size	Frequency
28	2
29	3
31	2
32	2
33	1

The mode is 29. It occurred the most often and in this case approximately three times. When there is one score that occurs most frequently in a distribution, we say the distribution is *unimodal* or, when graphed, it has one hump, because there is one mode.

Many frequency distributions have more than one mode. That is, more than one score turns up at the same high level of frequency. Two modes in a frequency distribution create a *bimodal* frequency distribution. This might occur in a set of data where two groups are performing very differently. If graphed, there would be two humps in the curve. For example, if "visits to the high school library" were measured for male and female freshmen, the distribution might be bimodal. In figure 3.3 there are two modes: 10 visits by males (or females) and 50 visits by females (or males).

Number of Library Visits	Tallies	Frequency (*f*)	
10	////////	8	**MODE**
20		0	
30	/	1	
40	/	1	
50	////////	8	**MODE**
60	//	2	
70	///	3	
80	//	2	
90	//	2	

Figure 3.3.   A bimodal distribution with two modes.

If there are more than two modes, the distribution is called *multimodal* and the graphing shows several humps or curves. Figure 3.4 shows what unimodal, bimodal, and multimodal frequency polygons look like when data sets have one, two, and three modes.

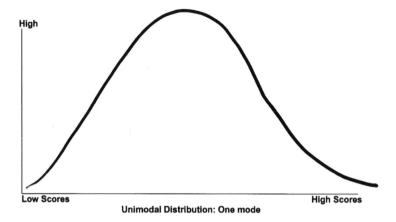

Unimodal Distribution: One mode

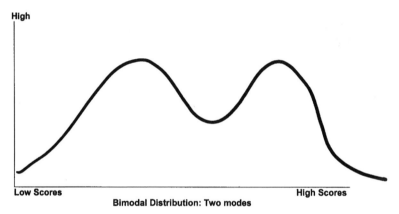

Bimodal Distribution: Two modes

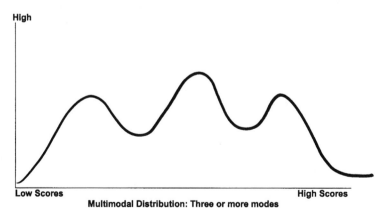

Multimodal Distribution: Three or more modes

Figure 3.4.   Frequency polygons: shapes of the unimodal, bimodal, and multimodal distributions.

CONCLUSION

Each measure of central tendency has a role to play in descriptive statistics. The mean is the preferred method of calculating the center of
your data set. But when outliers emerge, the median is an alternative
that is not affected by these unrepresentative scores. If you are in a
hurry and want to get a "ballpark feeling" for the average, the mode will
work with a quick glance at the frequency distribution table. Here is a
summary of the three measures and when to use which one. The best
advice is to report all three with an understanding of central tendency
and how each is derived.

The Mean
- If you want the greatest reliability
- If you will be calculating variability and other statistical computa-
  tions
- If your distribution has no outliers
- If your data are interval, ratio, and ordinal scaled

The Median
- If your distribution is skewed by outliers
- If your data are interval, ratio, or ordinal scaled

The Mode
- If you need a quick estimate
- If your data are nominal, ordinal, interval, or ratio scaled
- If you can "eyeball" the data from a frequency distribution

4

TELLING THE *WHOLE* STORY: VARIABILITY

From the last few chapters, we have learned how important it is to construct a frequency distribution and to go a step farther and plot the data into a graph for an immediate picture. Likewise, the value of the three measures of central tendency was established so that these measures could indicate to us with a single number the general character of our set of data. Each can suggest the typical profile of our set of scores.

Knowing our distributions and their central tendency is helpful but is not enough. The variability of the distribution is critical to discern. Unfortunately, statistics are often reported without mention of the *variance* or spread of scores. Think about how often newspapers report SAT or performance assessment data with *only the mean* as a statistic. This is a serious omission and even a misrepresentation of your data. This is why.

The variance is the manner in which your data are spread in either direction from the center of your distribution. It is important to know whether the scores tend to be quite similar (homogeneous) or whether they vary considerably (heterogeneous) from the center or mean/median/mode.

Whenever the measures of central tendency are reported in data sets, it is critical for educational leaders to report the variability. This is the amount of dispersion around the mean. The measures of variability tell us how representative our mean is. Are the scores the same or are they spread out?

For example, look at two sets of data for reading achievement in fourth grade.

Mrs. Doe's Grade 4	Mr. Smith's Grade 4
98	140
102	80
99	79
100	100
99	100
100	79
102	80
98	140
Mean = 100	Mean = 100

The mean in both cases is 100. Given that statistic, both fourth grades seem to be progressing in the same fashion. Closer inspection of the data shows that, while Mrs. Doe's class performed very much the same, Mr. Smith's class had some very high and very low scores. For Mrs. Doe's class the lowest score was 98 and the highest was 102. For Mr. Smith's class the lowest score was 79 while the highest was 140. The spread or dispersion was great in Mr. Smith's class, where there was high variability. Conversely, the low variability in Mrs. Doe's class was evident from the similar scores. There are practical implications for Mr. Smith that would be overlooked if just the mean were used to profile his classroom data.

There are several descriptive statistics that measure variability. The range, the variance, and the standard deviation, which are used often in educational settings, are discussed here.

THE RANGE

The *range* is a very simple statistic and the most unsophisticated measure of variability. In this regard, it possesses characteristics analogous to the mode in central tendency. It is a rough estimate, quickly computed but not tremendously stable. This is because it is computed with only two scores: the highest score and the lowest score in your distribution of scores. You subtract one from the other. The range for Mrs. Doe's class would be 4 (102 minus 98), while the range for Mr. Smith's class would be 61 (140 minus 79)! Even this crude measure of variability is very helpful in providing us with information.

The range is influenced by the size of your data set. The larger the data set, the greater the likelihood of extreme values because you have more potential for outliers. This is a limitation of the range; outliers affect it. Because you are using only two scores in your data set to calculate the range, if there is an outlier at either end, it will influence the calculation.

VARIABILITY AND GRAPHS

Graphs, discussed in chapter 2, are quite useful in initially determining the variability in your distribution. The *shape* of the frequency polygons and histograms that are constructed from the frequency distribution can tell us the story about the spread of scores at a glance. This is another asset of the frequency distribution (and their respective graphs) and a further reason to use them in getting to know your data set.

If the hump or curve in your graph is markedly flat, the scores are spread out; there is a great deal of variability. This type of curve is called *platykurtic,* and it means that your scores are spread out around the mean score of the distribution. On the other hand, if the hump or curve in your graph is peaked and tight, there is little spread in scores; the variability is low. This type of curve is called *leptokurtic,* and it means that your scores are very close to the mean score of the distribution. (See figure 2.4 in chapter 2, graphs D and E.)

Here are two graphs that display the number of books read by 11th grade students for two humanities courses during a special reading program. For both classrooms the mean number of books read was 6. As you can see, the students in history class read about the same number of books, while the number of books read by the English class varied. In fact, the range was 10 (11 minus 1) for the English class (figure 4.1) and only 4 (8 minus 4) for the history class (figure 4.2).

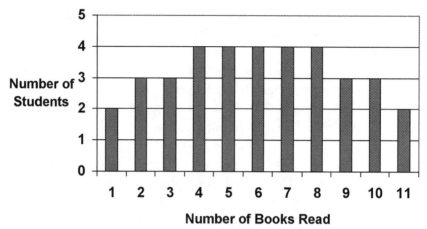

Figure 4.1.   Number of books read in English class.

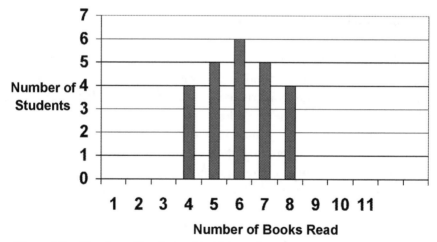

Figure 4.2.   Number of books read in history class.

The shape of the curves immediately indicates the dispersion or spread of scores. For the English class the shape of the curve is flat *(platykurtic)*. The message from the graph is that scores are spread out around the mean. It suggests that examining the data further may be wise. To claim that most students are reading six books would be false even though that is the mean. For the history class the shape of the curve is peaked *(leptokurtic)*. The mean is an excellent measure of central tendency because there is little spread. It would be safe to conclude that most students read about six books.

VARIANCE AND STANDARD DEVIATION

There are two additional measures of variability: the *variance* and the *standard deviation*. Both are much better indicators of dispersion in your data set of scores than the range is. This is because they use all of the scores in the data set in their calculation (just as the mean does). While the mode and the range have similar traits (quick, unsophisticated), the mean and the variance/standard deviation are very much alike (precise, reliable). They are the "kings of variability" as the mean is the "queen of central tendency." In addition, each of these statistics relies on more precise measurement scales, such as interval and ratio. Some educators use the ordinal scale, but there is a tradeoff in precision.

The formulas for calculating both the variance and the standard deviation can be found in any math or statistics book. However, if you are using a statistical software package, these will be calculated for you. Conceptually, each of these statistics is arrived at by determining how much each score in your data set deviates from the mean and then putting the deviation scores into a formula for computation. The variance is the standard deviation squared, and the standard deviation is the square root of the variance. So they are more or less "siblings" in the realm of variance. The symbol for reporting the variance is "sigma squared" (σ^2). The symbol for standard deviation is SD or sigma (σ). These symbols are what you might see in professional journals.

Because both the variance and standard deviation are calculated by deviations from the mean in your data set of scores, their value is tremendous. With one single number, you can tell whether most of the scores in your data set cluster closely around the mean or are spread out. The larger the standard deviation, the more spread out are your scores in your data set.

For example, let's consider the SAT. We know that the mean is 500 and the standard deviation is 100. These are "givens" based on norms developed over many years. Last year your juniors took the SAT verbal and got a mean of 600 and a standard deviation of 50. This year your juniors took the SAT verbal and got a mean score of 610 and a standard deviation of 120. The newspapers report a 10-point gain in your SAT verbal performance. Your scores rose 600 to 610. What appears to be good news for your school system is in fact a hidden problem. The standard deviation of 120 shows outlier scores have shifted the mean upward and artificially created the image that all of your scores were rising. While you can luxuriate in this good news this year, it puts a tremendous strain on you next year when you have to explain to the public why the scores are back down to 600. If the standard deviation were calculated in addition to the mean, there would be a more accurate presentation of your junior students' performance.

Sadly, this scenario is typically what happens in towns across America in the reporting of all standardized testing results. What is *not* reported is the standard deviation. This leaves schools vulnerable to public assessments based on a few points—up or down—in mean score performance. The media fuel the fire. Educational leaders, not savvy about this reporting deficiency, are at risk of being attacked by the taxpayers.

If school systems used both the mean and the standard deviation, they would not be criticized as much when there are a few point gains and losses. In this particular example, last year's juniors performed better on the SAT verbal. The standard deviation was smaller (50), and thus the mean score of 600 was better able to represent overall performance. This year, there was a huge standard deviation of 120. This means that although the mean was higher, it did not represent your juniors' performance as well. There was a spread of SAT verbal scores around the mean.

Here is a "golden rule" for data-driven decisions in educational settings: *Whenever you report the mean, you should report the standard deviation.* They are the statistically married couple. The standard deviation tells you a great deal—how representative your mean is as a measure of central tendency for your data set.

Look at the data for the *number of suspensions* from three middle schools in your school district.

Suspensions in Three Middle Schools	Mean per Year	Standard Deviation
Card Middle	60	2
Hebert Middle	60	1
Fitz Middle	60	15

At face value three middle schools in your district have the exact number of suspensions per year—60. So, you assume that this is typical or average. However, the standard deviations tell a very different story. For Card Middle School and Hebert Middle School the means are very representative of the yearly average for suspensions. The standard deviation is small for both. If you actually drew a frequency polygon from the frequency distribution data per year, these two schools would have leptokurtic curves. The values would be close to the mean.

But this is not true for Fitz Middle School. This school has a greater spread of suspensions around the mean of 60, as signified by the standard deviation of 15. The frequency polygon for Fitz Middle School data would be flat. And, actually, the median might be the better measure of central tendency in this case. At the very least, it would behoove smart administrators to examine both the mean and median before they made a policy on suspensions.

NORMAL CURVES OR NORMAL DISTRIBUTIONS

The standard deviation is one of the most valuable tools that educational leaders have at their disposal. One of its supreme uses, and where it plays a significant role, is in helping us to interpret test score performance. To fully understand its value, a discussion of *the normal curve* is necessary. (Some of the information about the normal curve should be memorized; that is how fundamental it is.)

Most of the data that we use in public education is thought to be *normally distributed.* When a graphed frequency distribution resembles a bell, it means that there are a few scores on either end of the hump or curve; most scores are in the middle.

AREA UNDER THE NORMAL CURVE

A normal distribution creates *a bell-shaped* curve or frequency polygon. These are some characteristics of the normal curve:

1. It has one mode (unimodal).
2. The mean, median, and mode are exactly the same.

3. It is symmetrical and bell shaped.

4. The two tails (ends of the curve) do not touch the abscissa (*x*-axis).

When you draw a normal curve, you observe these four characteristics. Because the mean, median, and mode are dead center, and the curve is symmetrical, the normal curve, drawn in most statistics books, has ordinates or vertical lines from the top of the curve to the baseline. When you look at the picture of a normal curve, visualize thousands of children standing under the curve; imagine faces looking at you. This is what the normal curve is representing—all scores of individuals who have taken whatever variables you are examining. Let's visualize a state-mandated performance test; we have loads of students standing underneath the curve (figure 4.3).

As you can see, most of the students are standing in the center, creating the huge hump. This is where the mean is. That makes sense, because the mean reports the central tendency of the students' scores. Then, you can see that as we move away from the center or mean, the number of students standing underneath the outer areas of the curve is fewer and fewer until we get to the tails of the curves and there are a couple of, yes, outliers standing around. This is a typical pattern of data. Most people attain very similar scores, and thus they fall close to the middle, hence the mean. Fewer perform dissimilarly to their group.

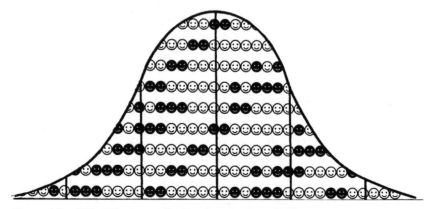

Figure 4.3.   What the normal curve represents—people.

THE TYPICAL GRAPH OF THE NORMAL CURVE

In the graph of SAT scores shown in figure 4.4, the vertical lines are drawn from the top of the curve to the baseline at zero and at numbers 1, 2, and 3 *to the left and to the right of zero.* Zero (0) represents the mean score or dead center. These vertical lines mark off areas under the curve and represent standard deviation units (1, 2, and 3) or distance from the mean. The standard deviation units act like a ruler and divide up the area under the normal curve.

The base of the normal curve is divided into six units with three standard deviations above and three standard deviations below the mean. Entries within the graph indicate the proportion of the total area (or number of scores) that fall into each of the six segments or demarcations. These are the proportions of area under the standard deviation cutoffs.

- Between the mean (0) and +1 SD units are 34.1% of all scores.
- Between the mean (0) and −1 SD units are 34.1% of all scores.

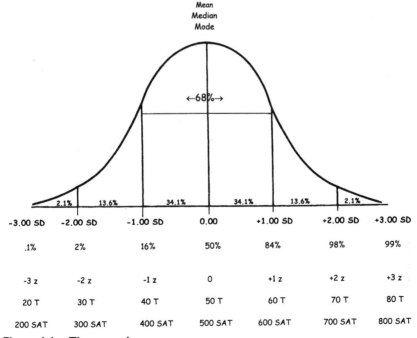

Figure 4.4.   The normal curve.

- Between ± 1 SD are 68% of all scores.
- Between +1 SD and +2 SD units are 13.6% of all scores.
- Between –1 SD and –2 SD units are 13.6% of all scores.
- Between ± 2 SD are 95% of all scores.
- Between + 2 SD and +3 SD units are 2.1% of all scores.
- Between – 2 SD and –3 SD units are 2.1% of all scores.
- Between ±3 SD are 99% of all scores.

Since we know that the mean is dead center, it is at the 50th percentile mark. The next bit of information is important to educational leaders in interpreting scores.

- *One standard deviation above the mean* is an area of 34%. This indicates that if your score is 1 SD above the mean, you performed better than 84% of all other scores in the distribution (50% plus 34%).
- *One standard deviation below the mean* is an area of 34%. This indicates that if your score is 1 SD below the mean, you performed better than only 16% (50% minus 34%).
- *One standard deviation above and below the mean* is an area of 68%. Over two thirds of the students perform within 1 SD of the mean (±1 SD). If you look at the normal curve and pretend again that students are standing underneath it, then this is very logical. It is where *most scores fall*, creating the large hump.
- *Two standard deviations above the mean* cover an area of 48%. Between the center (0) and +1 SD there is 34% of the area under the curve. Between +1 SD and +2 SD there is 14% of the area under the curve. As you can see, the farther you get from the center, the less area there is under the curve. This is because most scores/values are in the center where the hump is. Again, think of people standing underneath the curve.

If a student in your school gets a score that is 2 SD above the mean, he or she is in a select few. This student has performed better than 98% of all students (50% plus 48%).

- *Two standard deviations below the mean* cover an area of 48%. Between the center and –1 SD there is 34% of the area under the curve. Between –1 SD and –2 SD there is 14% of the area under the curve.

If a student in your school gets a score that is 2 SD below the mean, he or she is in the minority. This student has performed better than only 2% of all students (50% minus 48%).

- *Two standard deviations above and below the mean* is an area of 95%. If you look at the normal curve and pretend again that students are standing underneath it to create the hump in it, then the percentage of 95% is very logical. Almost all of the students perform within 2 SD of the mean (±2 SD).

The standard deviation units, together with the percentage of area under the normal curve, can be used to determine the relative position of scores above and below the mean. The information is defined as the "distance from the mean." This is extremely useful to educational leaders.

All standardized tests have means and standard deviations reported. Educational leaders thus can compare their entire school system or even an individual student's performance to the national norms. If there is a statewide test, you can be sure that mean and standard deviations by key segments exist for your comparisons. Or, you can calculate your overall district's mean and standard deviations and then compare individual schools to these baselines. Finally, you can calculate a mean and standard deviation for one segment of students and then compare individual student test scores to these.

The normal curve gives educational leaders the ability to make a call on where their school system, schools, or even individual students perform in relation to all others. This is because the percentiles under the normal curve indicate the relative position of those falling above and below a certain designation. Memorizing the distance from the mean and the percentile equivalents for the area under the curve is very worthwhile.

Here is a model that you can follow to set up a chart for any of your data sets. Substitute your own mean and your own standard deviation at each standard deviation unit. Then use the areas under the normal curve to pinpoint the performance levels you are trying to discern.

Calculations	−3 SD	−2 SD	−1 SD	0	+1 SD	+2 SD	+3 SD
from test→	(Mean −3 SD)	(Mean −2 SD)	(Mean −1 SD)	(Mean)	(Mean +1 SD)	(Mean +2 SD)	(Mean +3 SD)

The SAT serves as an easy example. We all have experience and are familiar with this test. For the SAT, the mean is 500 and the SD is 100. The vertical axis from the top of the normal curve to the mean divides the curve in half. This means that 50% of all test takers get around 500 as a score. We can infer that if they get a score of 400, they are 1 SD unit below the mean and performing similar to 16% of their peers. If they get 600, they are 1 SD unit above the mean and performing better than 84% of their peers. If they get a 700, they are in the advantaged minority. They are scoring 2 SD units above their peers and performing better than 98% of those taking the test. Conversely, a score of 300 means that they did better than only 2%. This is a great deal of information that you can obtain when you know the mean and standard deviation unit of any data set of scores—not just standardized tests.

As a bit of advice, educational leaders would be wise to calculate their own local norms (mean and SD) on the SAT. This would give you more reliable and valid data for your particular school system and not subject you to the misrepresentation of performance in the newspapers. Sometimes, a gain of two or three points on the SAT is viewed as a success, whereas a decline of two or three points is reported as a failure for local schools. This is a tremendous disservice, but few schools systems are armed with the correct data to present a truer picture.

If you have calculated your average SAT score and SD, you have your local baseline on which performance from year to year can be judged. You can do this retrospectively, too, because the data are in your records from past years. It is a matter of calculating means and standard deviations—time well invested.

A PRACTICAL EXAMPLE

Here is an example that demonstrates the practical utility of collecting this type of strategic information. Let's say that you decide to calculate the mean and SD for your junior-year students taking the SAT from the year 2000. Here is what you see:

Year	Mean	SD	±SD (68% of Scores)
2000	500	20	480–520
2001	500	60	440–560
2002	490	20	470–510

At first glance it looks as if your juniors took a dive in their SAT performance in the year 2002. They dropped from 500 in 2001 to 490 in 2002. This is a 10-point drop and one the media would report as a failure. However, you look at the standard deviations and note that a larger standard deviation unit (SD = 60) was obtained in 2001. This signifies that your 2001 juniors performed more heterogeneously than in previous years. Scores varied more around the mean. Conversely, the 2002 scores were very similar to those in 2000, when you consider the standard deviation. Scores were more like those in 2000 than in 2001.

If school leaders want to fortify themselves further, they would profile demographics on students who are taking the SAT from year to year. Their data-driven decisions should be asking questions such as, "Has the demographic composition of the test-taking student population changed?" For the hypothetical data just presented, it may be likely that in-migration has brought more diversity to your schools district in the year 2001. The diverse populations could account for the variability in scores. However, if you do not know the baseline information on both SAT performance and your local demographics, you cannot fully address the headline in your local newspaper that charges, "School is doing a poor job preparing students for college: SAT drops 10 points."

STANDARD SCORES OR Z SCORES

A *standard* or *z score* is another useful tool to educational leaders. Its symbol is lowercase "z." Standard scores describe a particular score's position in a distribution by expressing the score's distance above or below the mean. For example, if you knew a student's verbal score on a standardized verbal test, you could tell exactly where under the normal curve this student would be "standing." Then you could infer the level of that student's performance.

Here is how z scores work. You have a score on any given measure. As mentioned before, the symbol for a score is x. You calculate a z score by subtracting your score (x) from the mean and then dividing it by the standard deviation. This is your z score. If the z score is negative, then your standard score or z score is below the mean. If it is positive, it is above the mean. If it is zero, it is the mean.

The beauty of the z score is that you are able to find out exactly where under the normal curve you are. Most statistics books have a table that converts area under the normal curve from the mean ordinate to the z scores. A portion is displayed in figure 4.5. Here is how it is used.

Let's say that you achieved a z score of 1.34. You look in the table and it tells you that this z score corresponds to an area under the curve of 40.9%. This is highlighted so that you can see how it was located in the table. This would make sense, because we know that 1 SD is 34% and we have a z score that is *over* 1 SD. This is great information but made even better because we know that zero (0) is 50% in the normal curve. So we add the 40.9% from our z score with the 50% to create a percentage of 90.9%. We can conclude that our performance was 90.9% better than everyone else who took the test.

T SCORES

If you are writing a report, it may be better to go one step farther and transform the z scores into T scores. This artificial distribution has a mean of 50 and a standard deviation of 10. The formula is simple. Multiply your z score by 10 and add 50. That is your T score.

SD	−3	−2	−1	0	+1	+2	+3
T Scores	20	30	40	50	60	70	80

T score of 63 might be about here.

From the previous example, we had a z score of 1.34. To get a T score, we multiply it times 10 and get 13.4. Then we add 50 to obtain 63. If we know the mean is 50 and the standard deviation is 10 for T scores, we know where the score of 63 falls in the chart. It is above +1 SD.

z	.00	.01	.02	.03	.04	.05	.06	.07	.08	.09
0.0	.0000	.0040	.0080	.0120	.0160	.0199	.0239	.0279	.0319	.0359
0.1	.0398	.0438	.0478	.0517	.0557	.0596	.0636	.0675	.0714	.0753
0.2	.0793	.0832	.0871	.0910	.0948	.0987	.1026	.1064	.1103	.1141
0.3	.1179	.1217	.1255	.1293	.1331	.1368	.1406	.1443	.1480	.1517
0.4	.1554	.1591	.1628	.1664	.1700	.1736	.1772	.1808	.1844	.1879
0.5	.1915	.1950	.1985	.2019	.2054	.2088	.2123	.2157	.2190	.2224
0.6	.2257	.2291	.2324	.2357	.2389	.2422.	.2454	.2486	.2517	.2549
0.7	.2580	.2611	.2642	.2673	.2704	.2734	.2764	.2794	.2823	.2852
0.8	.2881	.2910	.2939	.2967	.2995	3023	.3051	.3078	.3106	.3133
0.9	.3159	.3186	.3212	.3238	.3264	.3290	.3315	.3340	.3365	.3389
1.0	.3413	.3438	.3461	.3485	.3508	.3531	.3554	.3577	.3599	.3621
1.1	.3643	.3665	.3686	.3708	.3729	.3749	.3770	.3790	.3810	.3830
1.2	.3849	.3869	.3888	.3907	.3925	.3944	.3962	.3980	.3997	.4015
1.3	.4032	.4049	.4066	.4082	.4099	.4115	.4131	.4147	.4162	.4177
1.4	.4192	.4207	.4222	.4236	.4251	.4265	.4279	.4292	.4306	.4319
1.5	.4332	.4345	.4357	.4370	.4383	.4394	.4406	.4418	.4429	.4441
1.6	.4452	.4463	.4474	.4484	.4495	.4505	.4515	.4525	.4535	.4545
1.7	.4554	.4564	.4573	.4582	.4591	.4599	.4608	.4616	.4625	4633
1.8	.4641	.4649	.4656	.4664	.4671	.4678	.4686	.4693	.4699	.4706
1.9	.4713	.4719	.4726	.4732	.4738	.4744	.4750	.4756	.4761	.4767
2.0	.4772	.4778	.4783	.4788	.4792	.4798	.4803	.4808	.4812	.4817
2.1	.4821	.4826	.4830	.4834	.4838	.4842	.4846	.4850	.4854	.4857
2.2	.4861	.4864	.4868	.4871	.4875	.4878	.4881	.4884	.4887	.4890
2.3	.4893	.4896	.4898	.4901	.4904	.4906	.4909	.4911	.4913	.4916
2.4	.4918	.4920	.4922	.4925	.4927	.4929	.4931	.4932	.4934	.4936
2.5	.4938	.4940	.4941	.4943	.4945	.4946	.4948	.4949	.4951	.4952
2.6	.4953	.4955	.4956	.4957	.4959	.4960	.4961	.4962	.4963	.4964
2.7	.4965	.4966	.4967	.4968	.4969	.4970	.4971	.4972	.4973	.4974
2.8	.4974	.4975	.4976	.4977	.4977	.4978	.4979	.4979	.4980	.4981
2.9	.4981	.4982	.4982	.4983	.4984	.4984	.4985	.4985	.4986	.4986
3.0	.4987	.4987	.4987	.4988	.4988	.4989	.4989	.4989	.4990	.4990

Figure 4.5. Percent of total area under the normal curve.

The z and T scores are calculated to get a sense of comparison. A savvy principal might take all standardized test scores for one grade level and calculate the mean and standard deviation. Then, z scores and T scores could be calculated for individual grades to compare performance. This information would be very beneficial.

In addition, the classroom teachers could use the data to compare individual student performance within their own classroom and between their classrooms and another of the same grade level. With the z and T scores, educational leaders can make some deductions that can stimulate follow-up action steps. Rather than viewing your performance test data as a report card only for the legislative and the public eye, make the data a workhorse toward real school improvement initiatives. This is the benefit of the normal curved distributions and percentage of area under the curve.

SKEWED DISTRIBUTIONS

Before closing this chapter, we need to address the fact that often our distributions or data sets are not normally distributed. When we use the statistics that will be discussed in the following chapters, there is an assumption that our data sets will be normally distributed. Many times they are, but sometimes they are not. We need to be able to identify distributions that are called *skewed*, or not normally distributed. (See figure 2.4 in chapter 2.)

Just as a review, *normal distribution curves* have the following characteristics:

- They are unimodal, having one mode only.
- The maximum height is at the mean where the zero (0) or vertical axis touches the top of the curve.
- The mean, median, and mode are equal.
- They are symmetrical and bell shaped. One half approximates the other half—a mirror image.
- There are one half of the scores on one side and one half on the opposite side of the mean.
- There are three standard deviations above and below the mean.

- They assume an infinite number of scores underneath the curve, so the two tails at either end do not touch the abscissa.
- They can be either platykurtic (flat) or leptokurtic (peaked), as well as in between.

On the other hand, we could have *positively or negatively skewed distributions*. How do we know? If scores are clustered near the middle in a frequency distribution with a few scores at the high and low ends, then it is pretty much a normal distribution. If there are concentrations of scores on either the high or low ends, then the distribution is skewed. Here are the hints:

- Our frequency distributions will confirm this because they will have outliers in them.
- The mean, median, and mode will not be equal.
- The frequency polygon will extend outward either left or right (the tails).

Positively Skewed Distributions

The *tail* of the curve tells you what kind of skew you have. If the tail is to the right, you have a *positively skewed curve*. With a positively skewed curve, the hump of the curve is toward the left. Remember when graphing frequency polygons, the left side of the horizontal axis begins with the lowest scores. Because the hump is in this vicinity, your distribution has many low scores. The few high scores, represented in the tail area, skew it. These "outlier" high scores pull the mean upward; the average is overrepresented. The mean *shifts* toward the outlier. In a positively skewed distribution, the mode is at the peak of the distribution. The mean is off to the right and the median is in between.

An example of a positively skewed distribution would be scores on a very difficult test where only a few students did well. The few who did well would be the scores on the tail and those who did not do well would be the large hump. An advanced placement exam might have this type of distribution. Sometimes, this type of curve exists when educational leaders are selecting a few students for a special program, such as a math enrichment program for budding engineers. Those in the tail of the curve would qualify or be selected because the program targets outliers—students with extremely high math aptitude.

Negatively Skewed Distributions

If the tail is to the left, you have a *negatively skewed curve*. With a negatively skewed curve, the hump or curve shows where most students' scores are falling. In this case they are at the higher end of the horizontal axis: the hump or curve is on the right side of the frequency polygon. The few low scores, represented in the tail area, skew it. These "outlier" low scores pull the mean downward; the average is underrepresented. The mean *shifts* toward the outlier. In a negatively skewed distribution, the mode remains at the peak, the mean is off to the left, and the median is in between.

An example of a negatively skewed distribution would be scores on a very easy test in which most did well. A driver's education exam should have a negatively skewed distribution. Most people pass it. This could also be the distribution of your middle school's mastery test scores when most should be passing. (Mastery test scores are *not* intended to be normally distributed. You want most students to master the content.) Negatively skewed distributions may be used to identify those students who need remediation. You would be looking at those scores in the tail to identify students with high levels of need.

CONCLUSION

Telling only part of the story about your data set occurs when measures for variance are missing. You are looking at part of the information puzzle but leaving off an important dimension. If data-driven decisions hinge on these descriptive statistics, then using both central tendency measures and measures of variation will be considered vital. Together, they will alert educational leaders to commonalities and differences that matter when taking action steps at the local level.

5

SAMPLES SAVE TIME

How many times do educational leaders wish that they could have a few more hours in the day, even a few more minutes? Time is at a premium in the public school setting. This is another advantage of using statistics. Although it probably was never conceived in this fashion, it is a tool for time management. Statistics allow you to build a foundation for data-driven decisions without spending many, many extra hours. Why is this so?

Statistics are based on *samples*. We have often heard this term batted around in the context of "random samples or scientific samples." Yet, few of us really know what this designation means and understand how valuable it is.

POPULATIONS AND SAMPLES

When we think of the term *population,* we usually think of people in our town, region, state, or country and their respective characteristics such as gender, age, marital status, ethnicity, religion, and so forth. In statistics, the term *population* takes on a slightly different meaning.

The *population* in statistics includes all members of a defined group that we are studying or collecting information on for data-driven decisions. The operative descriptor is "all"—all students, all grade levels, all faculty members, all parents, or the entire community of households in whatever geographic circle we are focused on. This could be our school district, our city or town, our region, our state, our nation, or the world. So the "population" in our statistical study is defined by the who (target group) and the where (the geographic boundary that this group exists in).

A *part* of the population is called a *sample*. Samples are studied to obtain valuable information about the larger group called the population. Once we define our population, we can take a sample of the population to conduct our statistics. A sample is a subset or subgroup of our population. It is a proportion of the population, a slice of it, a part of it and all its characteristics. A sample is a scientifically drawn group that actually *possesses the same characteristics* as the population—if it is drawn randomly. (This may be hard for you to believe, but it is true.)

Randomly drawn samples have two characteristics:

- Every person has an equal opportunity to be selected for the sample.
- Selection of one person is independent of the selection of another person.

We use samples all of the time to represent the whole. We take a sample of unusual food—maybe a bite or two—to see if it pleases our palate. We use a sample of a new dishwasher detergent that comes in the mail to see if it really works as well as the manufacturer says it does. We take a sample of employer references to see if our new recruit is as good as the application suggests. We visit a sample of classrooms to determine if new teachers are managing behavioral issues effectively. We sample some of the households in our community to see what our school's image is. The Internal Revenue Service is one of the heaviest users of samples. How do you think they determine whom to audit? Samples give them the means to represent the entire group of taxpayers in their mission to monitor our 1040 forms.

WHY SAMPLE?

Why not use the entire population to draw our conclusions? For most purposes we can obtain suitable accuracy quickly and inexpensively on information gained from a sample. Assessing all individuals may be impossible, impractical, expensive, or even inaccurate. It is usually not feasible to include an *entire* population in a study except if the number of those in our population is small and manageable. Furthermore, statistics make it unnecessary. A sign of ineptitude in data-driven decisions is using an entire population when a sample will provide the same results. You save money and time, make fewer mistakes, and achieve the same end. This is a customer-oriented, cost-effective benefit to your school.

What is great about random samples is that you can generalize to the population that you are interested in. So if you sample 500 households in your community, you can generalize to the 50,000 households that live there. If you match some of the demographic characteristics of the 500 with the 50,000, you will see that they are surprisingly similar. Technically, if you calculated a mean for these 500 randomly selected households and then draw another sample of 500 different households from the same population as the first, your mean scores would be the same. This is the beauty of random samples. If drawn scientifically, they represent the entire population that you are interested in.

Many doubting Thomases will still be skeptical about whether a sample can truly represent the population. This is understandable. Yet, if properly conducted, sampling does work. Think about all of the national polls during presidential elections in the United States. They do not survey *all* of the nation's households. Instead, a random sample is drawn and surveyed. The results are pretty accurate. If you would like to get a feeling for the size of samples that represent entire populations, please refer to the work of Krejcie and Morgan listed at the end of this chapter.

The chart below suggests the great benefit that randomly selected samples afford educational leaders. The larger the population size, the smaller the sample. However, for smaller samples, you must use almost the entire population. (Population size is noted by uppercase "N" and sample size by lower case "n.")

Random Sample Sizes (*n*) Required for Population (*N*) Representation

Population Size (N)	Sample Size (n)
50	40
100	80
500	217
1,000	278
1,500	306
3,000	341
5,000	357
10,000	375
50,000	381
100,000	384

Samples must be drawn according to scientific principles and with precision and accuracy. There is always a price: to have a *truly representative* sample, you need to pay the piper. But the process is quite simple and methodological. If you follow the steps, you will find that the characteristics of your population are the same as those of your sample. This is a good check on the validity of your sample: If the percentages on some of the demographics are known about your population, then the same demographics will appear in the sample. This is a good test and a very convincing piece of information for those doubting Thomases.

As a note, statistics conducted on populations are called *parameters* and are designated with Greek letters. Statistics calculated on samples are called *statistics* and have Latin or Roman letters ascribed to them.

STEPS FOR DRAWING SIMPLE RANDOM SAMPLES

There is a "method to the madness," and you must abide by the rules of the game in sampling for your sample to be representative of the population.

- The first step in drawing a random sample is to identify all of the members in your population. You must be able to list them in what is called a *sampling frame*. The frame should have the names without order to them and be nonoverlapping (no duplicates). Alphabetizing the list by surname is a way to ensure a random order in the sampling frame. (Your computer can sort alphabetically based on the last name if a surname is entered into a database as a separate field.) One reason that you need to ensure random order of names is that some lists cluster names by neighborhood location, housing type, income, or some other grouping. This would negatively affect their equal chance of being selected.

- Second, you must give each name an identification number. Start with "1" and continue.
- Third, you must decide what the size will be for your sample. You can use the table suggested by Krejcie and Morgan (1970) or whatever feels right for you (or your stakeholders) to believe in the results you obtain. As a rule of thumb, use as large a sample size as possible. Whenever you are calculating means, percentages, or other statistics, the population is being estimated. Statistics calculated from large samples are more accurate than those from small samples. Large samples give the principle of randomness a chance to work.
- Fourth, you need to get a *Table of Random Numbers*. Many are located at the end of statistical or mathematical textbooks. The Table of Random Numbers contains numbers generated mechanically so that there is no discernable order or system to them. Each digit gets an equal representation. The Table of Random Numbers consists of rows and columns of numbers arranged at random so that they can be used at any point by reading in any direction left or right, up or down.
- We are now ready to draw our random sample.

A SIMPLE EXAMPLE

Here is our sampling frame of 20 members of our population—let's say our fourth grade classroom. We want to draw a random sample of 5 students who will go on a special field trip with other fourth graders to meet the governor of our state. We have listed all 20 students in our fourth grade class in alphabetical order and assigned an ID number to each from 1 through 20.

Sampling Frame

ID	Name
1.	Alex
2.	Allen
3.	Allison
4.	Amelia
5.	Brett
6.	Deanna
7.	Ellen
8.	Emily
9.	Felice
10.	Juan
11.	Julia
12.	Kara
13.	Krista
14.	Mark
15.	Miguel
16.	Maura
17.	Olivia
18.	Racheal
19.	Rebecca
20.	Seth

We know that our largest ID number has two digits (20). So we are going to need a two-digit column in the Table of Random Numbers. We close our eyes and put our finger down anyplace in the Table of Random Numbers. This is our starting point. We have decided in advance whether we would use two digits going up, down, left or right. So we begin.

In figure 5.1, we have a sample from a Table of Random Numbers, just for the point of illustration. In boldface is our starting point of 37. We do not have an ID number that is 37 and so we proceed down . . . 37, 81, 89, and we come to 06.

ID number 6 is the first ID number that is within our band of between 1 and 20. This is the first member of our random sample and it is *Deanna*. We continue. . . 82, 56, 96, 66, 46 until we come up with the next ID, which is number 13, Krista. Our three last members of the sample are ID number 8 (Emily), ID number 5 (Brett), and ID number 4 (Amelia). We have five randomly selected students: Deanna, Krista, Emily, Brett, and Amelia.

53	74	23	99	67	61	32	28	69	84	94	62	67	86	24
63	38	06	86	54	99	00	65	26	94	02	82	90	23	07
35	30	58	21	46	06	72	17	10	94	25	21	31	75	96
63	43	36	82	69	65	51	18	37	88	61	38	44	12	45
98	25	37	55	26	01	91	82	81	46	74	71	12	94	97
02	63	21	17	69	71	50	80	89	56	38	15	70	11	48
64	55	22	21	82	48	22	28	06	00	61	54	13	43	91
85	07	26	13	89	01	10	07	82	04	59	63	69	36	03
58	54	16	24	15	51	54	44	82	00	62	61	65	04	69
34	85	27	84	87	61	48	64	56	26	90	18	48	13	26
03	92	18	27	46	57	99	16	96	56	30	33	72	85	22
62	95	30	27	59	37	75	41	66	48	86	97	80	61	45
08	45	93	15	22	60	21	75	46	91	98	77	27	85	42
07	08	55	18	40	45	44	75	13	90	24	94	96	61	02
01	85	89	95	66	51	10	19	34	88	15	84	97	19	75
72	84	71	14	35	19	11	58	49	26	50	11	17	17	76
88	78	28	16	84	13	52	53	94	53	75	45	69	30	96
45	17	75	65	57	28	40	19	72	12	25	12	74	75	67
96	76	28	12	54	22	01	11	94	25	71	96	16	16	88
43	31	67	72	30	24	02	94	08	63	38	32	36	66	02
50	44	66	44	21	66	06	58	05	62	68	15	54	35	02
22	66	22	15	86	26	63	75	41	99	58	42	36	72	24
96	24	40	14	51	23	22	30	88	57	95	67	47	29	83
31	73	91	61	19	60	20	72	93	48	98	57	07	23	69
78	60	73	99	84	43	89	94	36	45	56	69	47	07	41

Figure 5.1. Partial table of random numbers.

THE OLD WAY IS ACCEPTABLE, TOO

For such a small sample as this one, we could have done it the old-fashioned way by drawing five names out of a hat that had all 20 names in it. And you can draw a random sample that way instead of using the Table of Random Numbers. You simply put all names in a container and thoroughly mix them up. If you have 1000 names in the bowl and want a sample of 100, draw the first name out. That is the first person in the sample. Mix up the names. (If you don't do this, then the name at the bottom will have less of a chance of being selected.) After mixing, draw the next name and continue until you get 100. This works the exact same way as using the Table of Random Numbers and is useful if your sample is small.

OTHER USEFUL SAMPLING STRATEGIES

Simple random sampling is a pristine way to draw your sample. There are other sampling strategies that are very useful as well. Many books on sampling alone provide more in-depth information about the processes and the benefits. Here is a summary of a few procedures that educational leaders can consider.

Systematic sampling is an often-used sampling strategy and is cost effective. Again, you must have a population sampling frame list that is in random order and nonoverlapping. Determine both the size of the population and the size of the sample you want to work with. Then, divide the sample size (n) into the population (N) size to get your key number, symbolized as "k."

- For example, if you wanted to have a sample of 300 (n) and had a population of 1500 (N), the key number (k) would be 5.
- Then, you would randomly pick any number between 1 and 5. Let's say you picked "4." That is your first ID number. Whoever is ID number 4 is the first member of your sample from the list of 1500.
- Then, systematically add 5 (your key number) to the first ID number of 4 and you get number 9. ID number 9 is the second member of your sample.
- The next ID number is ID number 14, then ID numbers 19, 24, and 29 until you get your sample size up to the 300 you intended.

You might use systematic sampling to select a sample of households in your community for a community survey. The town hall might have the listing already available, in random order and with ID numbers in sequence. This saves you time and labor. If the town hall will give you a set of mailing labels, all the better.

Cluster sampling is exactly what its name implies. You randomly select clusters or groups in a population instead of individuals. This would work if a state wanted to sample all third graders on their writing skills. They would randomly select third grade classrooms from all third grade classrooms in the state. Each of those classrooms selected would have 100% of the students in that classroom in the sample. The sampling unit or cluster is the third grade classroom, not the individual student. Sometimes, this is a more practical effort than selecting individuals. Each member of the cluster has an equal chance of being selected. The random selection of the clusters provides estimates of the population. This is a good cost-reduction technique.

Stratified sampling is used when the population is heterogeneous and it is important to represent the different strata or subpopulations. There is a proportional representation of strata in the sample—proportional to the population strata. We divide the entire population into strata (groups) to obtain groups of people that are more or less equal in some respect. Then, we select a random sample from each stratum. This ensures that no group is missed and improves the precision of our estimates. This might be used with different ethnic groups if we wanted to ensure that our sample included a proportional representation of African Americans, Asians, and Hispanics in addition to the Caucasians that predominated in our demographic pool in the school.

Convenience samples, exactly what the name suggests, are often what we have to use because of reality. We cannot draw a sample, but we have a group that is accessible, is representative of our target population, and is just available to us. Instead of becoming purists and throwing out the chance for collecting data for decisions, use what you have with the honest acknowledgment that there are limitations. If you proceed to collect data with respect to some systematic, thoughtful process, it is better than throwing out the baby with the bath water. For example, you may survey parents who attend the annual parents' open house at your middle school. Your school system cannot afford to conduct a mailed survey to all parent households in your system. The open house provides an accessible and captive audience of parents from which you can extract some valuable information about perceptions, satisfaction levels, expectations, and needs.

CONCLUSION

Except when the population of interest is small, it is foolish to survey an entire population, with the sampling procedures available to educational leaders. By using simple random, systematic, cluster, stratified, or even convenience sampling procedures we can get a handle on what we need to know and save time and limited fiscal and human resources. One of the most important uses of samples is that they afford us the opportunity to make a decision without spending a fortune to do so. This is a wise investment for any public school system today.

NOTE

Krejcie, R.V., and D. W. Morgan. 1970. Determining sample size for research activities. Educational and Psychological Measurements 30:607–10.

6

STATISTICAL SIGNIFICANCE: MUCH ADO ABOUT NOTHING?

Descriptive statistics, which describe our data, are very useful to educational leaders when making data-driven decisions. Other statistics are also very useful, but they take a little more expertise in implementation. They are called *inferential statistics*. This is because we can draw conclusions or inferences from them.

Educational leaders have hypotheses, which are guesses or hunches that they believe to be true about their target populations of stakeholders. To tell whether they are true or false, they have to subject their hypotheses to a test. They draw a randomly selected sample from their population of interest, compute statistics on the sample, and test whether their hunch is true or false. The role of the sample, discussed in the previous chapter, is essential to the process and makes the task of inferring possible. The inferential statistics used to draw these conclusions include the *t*-test, one-way analysis of variance, chi square analysis, and correlational techniques, among many others. These four will be discussed in this primer because they are considered to be user-friendly, pragmatic, and applicable in educational settings.

HYPOTHESIS TESTING

Hypotheses are suppositions presumed to be true. Investigations by educational leaders that test well-conceived hypotheses can yield evidence of considerable importance. They can tell us whether we should switch from one instructional method to another. They can tell us the degree to which having breakfast impacts learning for elementary school students. They can tell us the value of getting more males to participate in extracurricular activities. They can tell us whether our mastery or standardized test scores are improving, declining, or staying the same from year to year. They can answer a lot of our critical questions and turn hunches into strategic information on which data-based decisions can be made.

Because of the importance of posing these hypotheses, it is crucial to accept those that are true and reject those that are false. But how do we do this?

Central to the discussion of inferential statistics is the concept of probability. When your statistical analysis reveals that the probability is rare that the statistical result is due to chance, we call this a statistically significant result. It means that our observed outcome is so unique that it could not have occurred by chance alone.

NONDIRECTIONAL AND DIRECTIONAL NULL HYPOTHESES

All research, whether it is in the classroom or in the laboratory, begins with the research question or hypothesis. It is always stated in the null (negative) and is called the null hypothesis. This is because you have to be able to prove something is indeed true. It is similar to the philosophy in the courtroom of proving someone guilty. A person is innocent until proven guilty. The onus of proof is on the educational leader to prove that the null hypothesis is true. Technically, the word "hypothesis" is a Greek word that means "an assumption subject to verification."

Basically, there are two types of null hypotheses. The first type tests for *differences*. Two null hypotheses that test for differences are presented here as an illustration of how to state them correctly. Corresponding examples follow each.

Null Hypotheses That Test for Differences

- There is *no difference* between two groups on variable *x* (as represented by their mean scores). *Example:* There is no difference between newly hired and seasoned teachers in their teaching competence.
- There is *no difference* among three or more groups on variable *x* (as represented by their mean scores). *Example:* There is no difference among Asian, African American, Hispanic, and Caucasian students with respect to the availability of computers at home.

Sometimes a null hypothesis for differences takes a courageous step and predicts the direction of the difference. This is called a *directional null hypothesis*. Instead of stating a nondirectional null hypothesis such as, "There is no difference in teaching competence between newly hired and seasoned teachers," you would state a directional null hypothesis as, "Teaching competence is greater for newly hired than for seasoned teachers." The basis for this *directional* guess should be your knowledge base, evidence in the professional literature, or your own experience; it would not be a superficial guess. You are actually stating which mean score will be greater when you calculate your statistics.

In this case, you really believe that seasoned teachers have more competence than the newly hired teachers do. Remember that the hypothesis must still be stated in the *opposite* of what you think is true. It has to be stated in the null, which you really think is false. Then you have to prove it to be false. When we accept the null (or fail to reject the null), we are saying that our results are not statistically significant and are due to chance. When we reject the null (or the null is false), we are saying that our results are statistically significant and due to factors or conditions other than chance.

Null Hypotheses That Test for Relationships

The second type of null hypothesis tests for *relationships* between two variables. One is presented here as a way to state it correctly, and there is a corresponding example:

- There is *no relationship* between variable *x* and variable *y*. *Example:* There is no relationship between the weather and voter turnout for a school budget referendum.

For practical utility, this book will focus on these two types of null hypotheses: those that test for differences and those that test for relationships. The discussion is going to be kept simple yet practical so that you can use this information in your school system.

PROBABILITY LEVELS

The term *probability* applies exclusively to a future event. Many events in life are inherently uncertain. Probability may be used to measure the uncertainty of the outcome of such events. Any event may or may not occur. If it is sure to occur, the probability is 1.00. If it will never occur, the probability is 0. A probability of .50 means the event should occur once in every two attempts or 50% of the time. So any event that may or may not occur has a probability of between 0 and 1.00.

Educational journals often state that the results are "statistically significant" or "the probability level is less than .05." This means that observed difference is likely to be real rather than easily explainable by chance. Although somewhat arbitrary, the significance level is the magnitude of error that one is willing to take in making the decision to reject the null hypothesis.

The conventional levels for rejecting the null hypothesis are either .05 or .01. One (.01) is more conservative than the other (.05) because with .01 you are less willing to have your results due to chance alone. You will accept only one time in 100 that your results were due to chance. A .05 level of statistical significance is more generous in accepting a statement as true. With this probability level you will accept five times in 100 that your results were due to chance. A really conservative probability level is .001. This may be used in scientific medical studies where life-and-death situations depend on lack of errors or results due to chance. In education the commonly accepted probability levels are .05 and .01.

As a note, you need to choose the probability level *a priori*. This is a Latin term meaning " in advance." You have to decide early on—before you collect your data—and accept it when your statistical testing is completed. It is unethical for us to choose the conservative .01 level and then find out that we would have had statistical significance if we were more liberal with a choice of .05.

TYPE I AND TYPE II ERRORS

The selection of probability levels comes with the chance of making errors. These are called Type I and Type II errors.

Type I Errors

A Type I error is when you reject the null hypothesis when it was actually true. We conclude falsely that there were differences when there were none. This can be embarrassing when someone else replicates our study and our results do not hold up!

Making a Type I error is based on the level of statistical significance. If you selected .05, then five times out of 100 your results will be due to chance. Unfortunately, you got one of the five times. A more conservative level is .01 where only one time out of 100 your results will be due to chance alone. A liberal level is .10, where you believe that 10 chance results out of 100 are OK with you. This level is not often selected in educational settings and can largely contribute to Type I errors.

Type I errors may be costly to your school. If you are thinking about revamping an instructional program (eliminating one and adding another), your decision based on a Type I error may use funds without cause. It can be very expensive in tax dollars—spending your budget and marring your image at the same time, only to have a new investment that is really ineffective. Your decision to change from the status quo was wrong. This may be avoided by using a more conservative level of statistical significance. This is advised if the decision has great implications for your school district.

Type II Errors

A Type II error occurs when you accept the null hypothesis when it was, in fact, false. We conclude that there are no differences when in fact there were! This is less costly in educational settings because you are maintaining the status quo. If you maintain the status quo, but have a new idea that really makes a difference, children can suffer. If you used a conservative probability level to determine if school breakfast had an effect on academic performance for your kindergarten class, you may be keeping kids hungry and having them learn less because of your error in design.

This is a chart that summarizes what happens.

	ACCEPT the NULL ↓	REJECT the NULL ↓
The hypothesis is true.→	You are right!	You committed a Type I error. Probability level is more liberal (.05).
The hypothesis is false.→	You committed a Type II error Probability level is more conservative (.01).	You are right!

As a note, the only way to know that you have a Type I or Type II error in your findings is through replication. All good studies are repeated to corroborate findings. This may not be feasible in educational settings, but trying to ensure good research practices "by the book" is always the goal and in everyone's best interest.

ONE-TAILED AND TWO-TAILED TESTS OF STATISTICAL SIGNIFICANCE

With nondirectional null hypotheses, educational leaders are only suggesting that there will be a difference in mean score results. Which of the means will be higher is not speculated on. In the case of a nondirectional null hypothesis, a two-tailed test of significance is used.

If there is a prediction of which mean will be higher and which will be lower, you state a directional hypothesis. A one-tailed test of significance is used.

Nondirectional null hypothesis→　Two-tailed test of significance
Directional null hypothesis→　One-tailed test of significance

This may seem like a lot of mumbo jumbo, but all it means is simply this: a directional hypothesis is a leap for someone to make. He or she is predicting which mean score of the groups that are being compared is higher or lower. (For example, the mean score of seasoned teachers will be higher than the mean score of newly hired teachers.) When you take this leap you are rewarded with a one-tailed test of statistical significance. What this means is that your ability to reject the null hypothesis is boosted or heightened. The ability to reject the hypothesis is called *power*—power to reject the null.

FACTORS CONTRIBUTING TO "POWER"

There are certain conditions where it is easier to reject the null hypothesis.

1. *If you use parametric statistics.* Parametric statistics are the elite statistics. They are more powerful than nonparametric statistics in rejecting the null hypothesis. However, they depend on meeting a few assumptions before you go ahead and use them. They work best if your distribution is not skewed but rather normal, bell-shaped, and symmetrical. The groups that you are comparing should have equal variances or spread. This is called *homogeneity of variance.*

   Parametric statistics that are discussed in this primer are *t*-tests, one-way analysis of variance, and Pearson Product Moment correlation techniques. These are more powerful tests to reject the null hypothesis. Also, they are described as *robust*, a statistical term that means that they can hold up even when the assumptions stated earlier are violated. Parametric statistics rely on the computation of means and standard deviations, which use interval and ratio scaling.

   Nonparametric statistics require very few assumptions before their usage. They do not require normal distributions or equal variances. They are based on ordinal or nominal measurement and are easier to compute. The formulas are less complex. They use frequency counts instead of complicated calculations. Because nonparametric statistics do not rely on means and standard deviations, they lack the precision that parametric statistics possess. In general, if you know that the data come from a population that is normally distributed, you should use the parametric test. If not, use the nonparametric test. In chapter 9, we will discuss chi square analysis as an essential nonparametric statistic for use in educational settings.

2. *If you use a directional hypothesis.* One-tailed tests (used with directional null hypotheses) are more powerful than two-tailed tests (used with nondirectional hypotheses).

3. *If you use large sample sizes.* These are more powerful than small sample sizes.
4. *If you use a more liberal probability level.* If you choose .05 instead of .01, your chance to reject the null hypothesis is greater.
5. *If you use superior measurement tools.* High reliability and validity are the attributes of good instruments.

STEPS: HYPOTHESIS TESTING OR IMPLEMENTING THE SCIENTIFIC PROCESS

The following four steps constitute the basis for scientific inquiry, hypothesis testing. This framework may be more conceptual than practiced because computer programs have taken some of the work out of the steps. Yet, it is risky, but common, practice for some schools to use high-powered statistical packages with very little understanding of the processes involved. Familiarity and awareness are essential for conducting any inferential statistical procedure. This primer is based on that premise and will present the inferential statistics in that spirit in the next four chapters.

Step One: State the Hypothesis in the Null Form.

The null hypothesis can test for either differences or relationships. If it tests for differences, the null hypothesis is either nondirectional or directional, but you must be aware of which type you are using.

Step Two: Select Your Level of Significance or Level of Probability, either .05 or .01.

- *.05* establishes a 95% confidence level and is more liberal.
- *.01* establishes a 99% confidence level and is more conservative.

Step Three: Compute Your Statistical Analysis.

Determine whether you have a statistically significant result. (How this is done will be discussed in detail in the next chapters.)

- *No* statistically significant result: Accept your null hypothesis as true.
- *Yes*, a statistically significant result: Reject your null hypothesis as false.

Step Four: Determine the Educational Significance of Your Results.

Is the statistical difference meaningful? Or is this a "so what?" finding? Concerning the last step, don't let your ego overtake common sense.

Wise educational leaders must look beyond statistical significance when making data-driven decisions and ask themselves, "Is this educationally significant?" Is the difference between the two or more mean scores large enough to be worth the cost of changing programs, eliminating programs, or adding programs? How important is the difference? How much better can this finding make our program or school? Is the change worth it? What is the cost-effectiveness? Are the gains in student scores large enough to invest to obtain this difference? This is the last step in hypothesis testing and one in which we have to put our egos aside to answer for the good of our schools.

A final thought is in order regarding statistical significance. Everyone seems to think that getting a statistically significant result is the "gold ring." This is not always the case. It depends on what you are asking in your evaluation or research study. For example, if you want to know if males and females have different attitudes toward your faculty, you would like to think there was no significant difference. If you were asking whether there were differences in teaching expertise between newly hired and tenured teachers, you would like to think there was none.

CONCLUSION

The use of inferential statistics in educational settings allows us to make strategic decisions based on data. We avoid guessing, speculating, and listening to the squeaky wheels about what is effective, what is not, what should stay in the budget, what should be eliminated, what should be added or expanded, and what should be changed or modified. Inferential statistics go a long way toward supplying the foundation for smart decisions. There is a price. A "method to the madness" must be observed. There is a scientific nature to hypothesis testing and principles that must be respected. But it is a small price to pay for what schools get in exchange.

7

TESTING YOUR HUNCH ABOUT DIFFERENCES: *T*- TESTS

For educational leaders, data-driven decisions are often focused on comparisons:

- Methods of instruction, to see which impacts performance
- Athletic programs, to determine which is more cost-effective
- Professional staff, to measure the impact of professional development
- Elementary schools, to compare standardized test performance

When two groups are compared, the statistic that is most useful in data-driven decisions is very often the *t*-test. It is an inferential statistic.

The purpose of a *t*-test is to determine if there is a statistically significant difference between the mean scores of two groups. This is where the mean, the "queen of central tendency," is vital. The mean scores of two groups are compared with the formula for a *t*-test. Because the *t*-test is a parametric statistic, it is powerful. If there are differences, even slight ones, the *t*-test will uncover them.

Here are a few basic facts about *t*-tests:

1. A *t*-test is used if there are only *two* groups to compare.
2. This statistical technique answers the null hypothesis: There *is no difference* between two groups on their respective mean scores.

3. There is one independent variable with two categories, and there
   is one dependent variable.

INDEPENDENT AND DEPENDENT VARIABLES

There is much confusion around what constitutes independent and dependent variables. To understand the difference is fundamental to exe-
cuting statistics properly. This is where the use of a "canned" statistical
software package can be dangerous if you are not aware of even the basic content presented in this primer. The simplicity of the "click, click"
of the computer mouse superficially and dangerously erases the need to
know. But understanding which one is the dependent variable and
which one is the independent variable is vital to producing correct statistical analysis for data-driven decisions.

Basically, the *independent variable* for a t-test is nominally scaled. There
are two discrete categories with one variable. It is that simple. Many educators think that because there are two categories there are two independent variables. There is only *one* independent variable with a t-test and it
has two categories. The chart below presents a few examples.

Independent Variable	Group One Category	Group Two Category
High school seniors	College bound	Employment bound
Fourth graders	Special education	General education
Seventh graders	Participants in athletics	Nonparticipants in athletics
Gender	Males	Females
Marital status	Married	Not married
Faculty	Mathematics	Language arts
Parents	Registered voters	Not registered voters
School staff	Paraprofessionals	Professionals
Community	Year-round residents	Summer-home residents

To nominally scale these independent variables for statistical analysis
in a t-test, you can assign a "1" to one group and a "2" to the other. Remember, with nominal variables the numbers are only labels. They

mean nothing in terms of measurement but everything in differentiating the categories of your independent variable.

A *t*-test has only one dependent variable. It is continuous in its numeric range and uses interval or ratio measurement scales. Sometimes, educators will use ordinal scales; this is not the perfect scenario given the parametric nature of the *t*-test, but the practice is common and acceptable. (See chapter 1 for a refresher on the different measurement scales.)

Common examples of dependent variables in educational settings are standardized test scores, numbers of suspensions or absences, dropout rates, parent satisfaction levels, organizational climate, and student performance.

PRELIMINARY ASSUMPTIONS

Parametric statistics were described in chapter 6. This group of statistics is more powerful than nonparametric statistics in rejecting the null hypothesis. Because the *t*-test is a parametric statistic, there are a few preliminary assumptions that you must undertake before you implement this statistical procedure.

- *The two groups should have equal variances on the dependent variable.* The variability (discussed in chapter 4) of the individual groups' mean scores must be equivalent. They must have the same degree of variability. This is called a test of homogeneity of variance and should be done as a preliminary step, a kind of insurance program for your data. This is particularly true when your groups are of different size (*n*), which is common in educational settings (versus laboratory settings where things are "perfect").
- *The two groups should have an equal number of subjects.* If the two groups are unequal, such as 20% more scores in one group than in the other, look at the standard deviation. If they are similar, go ahead and use the *t*-test. If they are not, use the Mann-Whitney *U* test, a nonparametric counterpart discussed at the end of this chapter.
- *Groups should be equivalent on all other variables except the dependent variables.* For example, if you are examining instructional approaches in two elementary schools by comparing student test

scores, make sure that the two elementary schools are similar on other characteristics. These might include income of the households that compose the feeder neighborhoods, percentages of students in special education, and other factors that may account for differences in test scores between the two schools instead of your focus—instructional approach.

In your effort to meet the assumptions of the *t*-test, keep in mind that *t*-tests are "robust." They can hold up even when the assumptions, just stated, are violated. Although this "robustness" lets us off the hook in doing pristine research, it is a good idea to approximate to the greatest extent possible the rules of the game. This will ensure excellent data management, avoid errors, and ultimately produce sound data-driven decisions.

WALKING THROUGH THE STEPS FOR CONDUCTING A *T*-TEST

This example will help to explain the basic purpose of the *t*-test. You are the principal of a large school with 30 math teachers. Let's say that your state had a test to assess teachers' mathematics knowledge. There was new mathematics content for students, and it was mandated by the state performance standards. Your newly hired teachers and those teaching for more than 10 years (called "seasoned" for the purpose of illustration) were compared on their scores. You wondered if there was a difference between the two groups. This would have important implications for professional development if it were found to be true. So you decide to compare the overall mathematics scores between the two groups of teachers.

Step One: You State Your Null Hypothesis. It Is Nondirectional.

There is no difference in mathematics knowledge between newly hired and seasoned teachers.

Step Two: You Identify Your Independent Variable and Your Dependent Variable.

"Teachers" was your independent variable with two categories: newly hired teachers and seasoned teachers. You took the listing of all of your teachers and separated them by years of teaching into the two groups. Group one included *newly hired teachers* and group two was composed of *seasoned teachers*. Using nominal scaling, you assign each group a numeric label so that your *t*-test could be calculated. You used "1" and "2" as your numeric values, which represented the two categories of teachers.

Your dependent variable was mathematics knowledge, as measured by the state's test. You listed the score for each teacher on the math test. You also calculated the mean scores for each of the two groups. The mean scores appeared different, but you could not really tell just from "eyeballing the data." A *t*-test formula had to be applied to the data.

Step Three: You Set Up Your Data for Data Entry into a Database.

The data for your *t*-test was recorded in a database such as that in figure 7.1. As a note, you will be using *only the numeric values* in your database, that is, the teachers' ID numbers, the group codes, and the mathematics scores for each of the 30 teachers. This way, the name of the teacher is preserved for confidentiality. You have data on 15 newly hired and 15 seasoned teachers.

Step Four: You Execute the t-test Statistical Procedure to Obtain a Calculated t Value.

After you have entered your data from your database into the computer software program of your choice, you can execute the *t*-test procedure. You can also hand-calculate the *t*-test by using a formula found in any statistics or mathematics textbook. Either way, what will be the outcome is a *t* value. It is called your calculated *t* value.

For the sample data, your calculated *t* value actually is –4.97. This calculated *t* value is theoretically the calculated difference in your two mean scores in mathematics for the two groups of teachers. It is critical to your decision whether to reject or accept the null hypothesis. The *t* value is a continuous number usually with two decimal places. The plus or minus sign in front of the *t* value does not matter; ignore it.

ID	Teachers	Category N = 30	Group code	Mathematics Score
1.	Mr. Ramirez	New	1	88
2.	Ms. Olsen	New	1	89
3.	Ms. Kurker-Stewart	New	1	88
4.	Mrs. Van Koten	New	1	89
5.	Mr. Busch	New	1	76
6.	Ms. Marchand	New	1	89
7.	Mr. Hoffman	New	1	88
8.	Ms. Loffler	New	1	89
9.	Mrs. Gallagher	New	1	88
10.	Ms. Magistrali	New	1	89
11.	Ms. Strand	New	1	89
12.	Mr. Krafcik	New	1	88
13.	Ms. Bowen	New	1	89
14.	Ms. Seymour	New	1	88
15.	Mrs. Pacheco	New	1	89
	Mean for Group One	15 = n		87.73

ID	Teachers	Category N = 30	Group code	Mathematics Score
16.	Ms. French	Seaoned	2	89
17.	Mr. Dickinson	Seasoned	2	78
18.	Mrs. Adazzio	Seasoned	2	75
19.	Ms. Saidel	Seasoned	2	78
20.	Mr. Dwyer	Seasoned	2	79
21.	Ms. Wallace	Seasoned	2	89
22.	Ms. Calafiore	Seasoned	2	78
23.	Mrs. Kozlak	Seasoned	2	75
24.	Mr. Fitz	Seasoned	2	78
25.	Ms. Hernandez	Seasoned	2	79
26.	Ms. Torsiello	Seasoned	2	78
27.	Mrs. Santo	Seasoned	2	75
28.	Mr. Adams	Seasoned	2	78
29.	Ms. Vega-Perez	Seasoned	2	79
30.	Mr. Hebert	Seasoned	2	70
	Mean for Group Two	15 = n		78.53

Figure 7.1. Two groups of teachers and their mathematics data for the t-test.

Step Five: You Compare Your Calculated *t* Value to the Critical *t* Value in the *t* Distribution Table.

You have to compare your calculated *t* value to what is called the critical *t* value reported in the *t* distribution table usually found at the end of any research or statistics book. A portion of this table is displayed in figure 7.2. To use this table correctly you have to know three pieces of information:

- Was your null hypothesis a nondirectional (two-tailed test) or a directional (one-tailed test) one?
- What was the level of probability that you selected? .05? or .01?
- Did you use an independent or correlated *t*-test that determines the degrees of freedom (*df*)? (This is discussed in more detail, shortly.)

If the calculated *t* value exceeds (is higher than) the critical *t* value in the *t* distribution table, you reject the null hypothesis. You have a statistically significant difference. If not, you accept the null hypothesis as true. For your data set, the calculated *t* value was 4.97. Because you had a nondirectional hypothesis, a probability level of .05, and an independent *t*-test (*df* = 28), the critical value in the *t* distribution table was 2.048. (It is highlighted in figure 7.2 so that you can see how it was located.) Your calculated value of 4.97 exceeded the table value.

Step Six: You Accept or Reject the Null Hypothesis.

Your calculated value exceeded the table value. You reject the null hypothesis.

There is a difference in mathematics knowledge between newly hired and seasoned teachers.

You found that your newly hired teachers had statistically higher mathematics scores. When you have a statistically significant finding, you report it with an asterisk. One asterisk (*) indicates that the probability level was .05, two asterisks (**) signify a probability level of .01, and the notation of NS usually stands for not statistically significant.

This *t*-test finding motivated you, as the educational leader, to implement professional development in areas where seasoned teachers

df	Two-tailed test at P < .05	Two-tailed test at P < .01	One-tailed test at P < .05	One-tailed test at P < .01
1	12.706	63.657	6.314	31.821
2	4.303	9.925	2.920	6.965
3	3.182	5.841	2.353	4.541
4	2.776	4.604	2.130	3.747
5	2.571	4.032	2.015	3.365
6	2.447	3.707	1.943	3.134
7	2.365	3.499	1.895	2.998
8	2.306	3.355	1.860	2.896
9	2.262	3.250	1.833	2.831
10	2.228	3.169	1.812	2.764
11	2.201	3.106	1.796	2.718
12	2.179	3.055	1.782	2.681
13	2.160	3.012	1.771	2.650
14	2.145	2.977	1.761	2.624
15	2.131	2.947	1.753	2.602
16	2.120	2.921	1.746	2.583
17	2.110	2.898	1.740	2.567
18	2.101	2.878	1.734	2.552
19	2.093	2.861	1.729	2.539
20	2.086	2.845	1.725	2.528
21	2.080	2.831	1.721	2.518
22	2.074	2.819	1.717	2.508
23	2.069	2.807	1.714	2.500
24	2.064	2.797	1.711	2.492
25	2.060	2.787	1.708	2.485
26	2.056	2.779	1.706	2.479
27	2.052	2.771	1.703	2.473
28	2.048	2.763	1.701	2.467
29	2.045	2.756	1.699	2.462
30	2.042	2.750	1.697	2.457

Figure 7.2.   Distribution table for t values.

needed updating. The newer math principles were not taught at the postsecondary level for your seasoned teachers. You addressed this by designing seminars to be taken during the next school year. That was the practical action step that resulted from your t-test. A t-test was how you arrived at this data-driven decision.

INDEPENDENT AND CORRELATED T-TESTS

Although this primer is intended to keep things as simple as possible, there is a critical addendum to the t-test discussion. There are two forms of the t-test. One is called the independent samples t-test, and the other is called the correlated samples t-test, also referred to as a paired or matched samples t-test. To use the distribution table for t values correctly, you need to know whether you conducted an independent or correlated samples t-test.

The independent samples t-test is quite simple to understand and identify. The two groups, such as new and seasoned teachers, have *no relationship* to each other. They are independent of one another, hence the name independent samples t-test.

Conversely, correlated samples t-tests use two groups that have a connection or relationship to each other. With this built-in relationship, it is more likely that the mean scores of the two groups have a relationship, too. So, the correlated samples formula takes the inherent relationship into account and helps to find a statistical significance, if there is one. Here are the occasions when you are using a correlated t-test:

1. *When you have two sets of scores on the same individuals*—in other words when the individuals are tested twice. Two groups of data are really the same individual with two scores on each person. The chart below displays an example in which the students are each measured twice. For each student, the pair or dual scores compose the two groups of data needed for a t-test.

	Pre-test	Post-test
Maria	120	140
Joe	120	120
Annie	130	160
Erica	150	160

Correlated *t*-tests are used most often in educational settings for this purpose. It is of great benefit to educational leaders who want to determine impact, efficacy, and persistence over time. Some examples of when correlated *t*-tests might be used include the following:

- When assessing the ability of a new instructional method to raise standardized test scores
- When measuring the impact of an innovative program on students' attitudes
- When weighing the cost benefit of a novel approach on remediation
- When tracking community support from last year to this year
- When monitoring the effect of professional development training on knowledge acquisition

2. *When you have sets of twins that compose the two groups.*

    More often in laboratory settings, but sometimes in educational settings, sets of twins are used to compose the two groups. This is because they are genetically similar. Then, data are collected on each twin and the *t*-test is conducted between the data for twin group A and twin group B to see if statistical differences exist. Because the two groups of twins are obviously related, the correlated *t*-test is used. The following chart shows how twins would be split into the two groups for data analysis on IQ scores.

Group A	IQ Score	Group B	IQ Score
Adams Twin A	120	Adams Twin B	122
Ruoz Twin A	133	Ruoz Twin B	134
Houle Twin A	125	Houle Twin B	123
Arum Twin A	134	Arum Twin B	134

3. *If you have matched your sample on some other variable so that the two groups are alike.*

    One of the primary tenets of the *t*-test is that the two groups you are studying are alike *except* for your dependent variable. You want to ensure that something else (called extraneous variance or error) does not account for differences between the two groups instead of your dependent variable.

For example, look at the data set of teachers discussed previously. What might account for the difference in mathematics knowledge besides whether a teacher is new or seasoned? The answers might be type of university training, amount of professional development, confidence with subject area, attitude toward profession, institutions that granted their degrees, or other factors. If there were one particular factor that you believed might compromise your data, you might try to match the groups on that variable, so that they are equivalent except for the dependent variable you were exploring.

MATCHED SAMPLES

Here is an example of a matched sample. Using the same set of data that we used in your *t*-test, the two teacher groups were matched on number of professional development courses they have taken. As you can see in figure 7.3, each teacher in group one is matched with another teacher in group two on the number of professional development courses that they took. For each ID number in group one there is a member of group two that has the same number of professional development courses. Mr. Ramirez was paired with Ms. French, Ms. Olsen with Mr. Dickinson, and all the way through there were pairs of teachers with the same number of professional development courses in each of the two groups.

The number of professional development courses would not be entered into the *t*-test that you were calculating. It would just ensure that your groups of teachers were equivalent on this important variable (number of professional development courses) before you began to compare mathematics knowledge. Your null hypothesis is still focused on the variable "years as a teacher" and its impact on mathematics knowledge—not the number of professional development courses.

ID	Teachers	Professional Development Courses	Category	Group Code	Mathematics Score
1.	Mr. Ramirez	1	New	1	88
2.	Ms. Olsen	1	New	1	89
3.	Ms. Kurker-Stewart	2	New	1	88
4.	Mrs. Van Koten	3	New	1	89
5.	Mr. Busch	4	New	1	70
6.	Ms. Marchand	1	New	1	89
7.	Mr. Hoffman	4	New	1	88
8.	Ms. Loffler	5	New	1	89
9.	Mrs. Gallagher	3	New	1	88
10.	Ms. Magistrali	4	New	1	89
11.	Ms. Strand	5	New	1	89
12.	Mr. Krafcik	1	New	1	88
13.	Ms. Brown	2	New	1	89
14.	Ms. Seymour	2	New	1	88
15.	Mrs. Pacheco	3	New	1	89

ID	Teachers	Professional Development Courses	Category	Nominal Scale	Mathematics Score
1.	Ms. French	1	Seasoned	2	89
2.	Mr. Dickinson	1	Seasoned	2	78
3.	Mrs. Adazzio	2	Seasoned	2	75
4.	Ms. Saidel	3	Seasoned	2	78
5.	Mr. Dwyer	4	Seasoned	2	79
6.	Ms. Wallace	1	Seasoned	2	89
7.	Ms. Calafiore	4	Seasoned	2	78
8.	Mrs. Kozlak	5	Seasoned	2	75
9.	Mr. Fitz	3	Seasoned	2	78
10.	Ms. Hernadez	4	Seasoned	2	79
11.	Ms. Torsiello	5	Seasoned	2	78
12.	Mrs. Santo	1	Seasoned	2	75
13.	Mr. Adams	2	Seasoned	2	78
14.	Ms. Vega-Perez	2	Seasoned	2	79
15.	Mr. Hebert	3	Seasoned	2	70

Figure 7.3.   Matched groups of teachers and their mathematics data for the t-test.

USING THE *T* DISTRIBUTION TABLE CORRECTLY: DEGREES OF FREEDOM

The reason that you must know whether you used an independent samples or correlated samples *t*-test is because of the *t* distribution table. To use the *t* distribution table correctly, you must know what your degrees of freedom are. This is a prerequisite for using most statistical tables. There is a column where *df* is noted so that you can find the critical value. In this case of the *t*-test, it is the critical *t* value.

Independent samples and correlated samples have different "degrees of freedom" associated with each form.

- If you use an independent samples *t*-test, the degrees of freedom are equal to the number in your total sample minus 2 or $(N - 2)$. So in the first example of new and seasoned teachers, the degrees of freedom would be 28 (or 30 teachers minus 2 = 28). For a nondirectional hypothesis (two-tailed test) at the .05 level with 28 degrees of freedom, your calculated *t* value had to exceed 2.048, the actual critical value in the *t* distribution table. It did, with a *t* value of 4.97.
- If you are using a correlated samples *t*-test, the degrees of freedom are equal to the number of pairs minus 1 (N of pairs – 1). In the second example of teachers, you used matched pairs on professional development courses; the degrees of freedom would be 14 (or 15 pairs – 1). For a two-tailed test at the .05 level with 14 degrees of freedom, the critical value your calculated value must exceed is actually 2.145.

As you can see, the critical value for the correlated samples *t* is higher than that for the independent samples *t*. This makes it more difficult to reject the null hypothesis. Because the data for the groups are related, you have to ensure that the difference you find is real and not due to the relationship between the sets of data. So the bar is raised with correlated samples *t* tests.

REPORTING *T*-TEST RESULTS IN A TABLE FORMAT

Figure 7.4 shows how you might report your *t*-test findings in a table format in your report to the board of education.

Independent Samples *T*-test

Teachers' Groups	Mean	(SD)	t Value	df	P
Newly Hired Teachers	87.33	(4.9)	4.97	28	.05*
Seasoned Teachers	78.53	(4.9)			

*P<.05

Correlated Samples *T*-test

Teachers' Groups	Mean	(SD)	t Value	df	P
Newly Hired Teachers	87.33	(4.9)	4.97	14	.05*
Seasoned Teachers	78.53	(4.9)			

*P < .05

Figure 7.4.   T-test tables.

NONPARAMETRIC COUNTERPARTS

There are two nonparametric statistical procedures that answer the same question that the *t*-test does. If the assumptions mentioned in the beginning of this chapter cannot be met, then you may want to consider using a nonparametric alternative. The Mann-Whitney *U* test and the Wilcoxon Matched-Pairs Signed-Ranks test are the counterparts to the independent samples and correlated samples *t*-tests, respectively. They are not bound by normal distributions or equal variances. They can be used with ordinal data or ranked data instead of interval/ratio scaling for the dependent measure. The downside is that they are not as powerful as the parametric *t*-tests in rejecting the null hypothesis.

CONCLUSION

The *t*-test is a very useful tool in educational settings. Often we are comparing two methods, two programs, two groups of students, or two groups of stakeholders to make a decision. The *t*-test is a simple and straightforward statistic that allows us to get beyond a frequency count. A group's mean score may look different from another mean score, or it may look the same. The litmus test for two group comparisons is called the *t*-test. It is a tool that educational leaders can use to make decisions confidently and then take the appropriate action based on the results.

8

TESTING YOUR HUNCH ABOUT DIFFERENCES: ANOVA

The *t*-test is very handy when educational leaders have two groups to compare. But what happens if you have more than two groups? The statistical technique that is analogous to the *t*-test is called *analysis of variance*, or *ANOVA*. The purpose of the ANOVA is understood quickly if it is thought of as an extension of the *t*-test.

The ANOVA is an inferential statistic. It is also a parametric statistic and is very powerful. It can reject the null or find differences among groups—if indeed they exist. The assumptions of homogeneity of variance, equal group sizes, and normal distribution of scores should be adhered to—just as the *t*-test should meet these assumptions. Yet, as a robust statistic, ANOVA can sustain having the assumptions violated and still perform its function. There is a nonparametric version of the ANOVA called the Kruskal-Wallis *H* test. If you have serious violations of the assumptions, use it.

Frankly, ANOVA is more complicated than a *t*-test and may require some outside expertise to execute and to interpret it (even with a "canned" statistical package). For the purpose of discussion, the main point is that you use ANOVA as you do a *t*-test—when there are more than two groups. Although there are many versions of the ANOVA, in this primer the focus is on a simple version: the one-way ANOVA.

Here are some facts about one-way ANOVAs:

- This statistical technique answers the null hypothesis: There is *no difference* among three or more (3+) groups on their respective mean scores.
- There is one independent variable with three or more (3+) categories. These levels are nominally scaled. (As a note, you *can* use an ANOVA to compare two groups, too, but the *t*-test is intended for that purpose.)
- There is one dependent variable that is continuous in its numeric range. This means that interval or ratio scales (where units are exactly the same) are used.
- The statistic you obtain to determine statistical significance is the *F ratio* or F statistic.
- The distribution table in the statistics books is called the F distribution table.

WALKING THROUGH THE STEPS FOR CONDUCTING A ONE-WAY ANOVA

An example will help to explain the basic purpose of the one-way ANOVA. As superintendent of schools, you are hoping that your budget referendum gets passed because you need to hire more staff, institute a new reading program, and buy updated textbooks for the middle school. The taxpayer backlash has been ruthless. So you consider implementing a public relations campaign using parent leaders as image emissaries. But do all parents in the community support the school system to the same degree? To find out, you conduct a community survey of parent leaders.

Step One: You State Your Null Hypothesis.

There is no difference in levels of support among elementary, middle, and secondary school parents.

Step Two: You Identify Your Independent Variable and Your Dependent Variable.

"Parents" was your independent variable with three categories: elementary, middle, and secondary school parents. You took the listing of your parent households and separated them by the three groups.

- Group one was the elementary school group.
- Group two was the middle school group.
- Group three was the secondary school group.

Using nominal scaling, you assigned each parent group a numeric label so that your ANOVA could be calculated. You used "1," "2," and "3" as your numeric values, which represented the three categories of parent groups.

Your dependent variable was "school support." You listed the total numeric score on the community survey for each parent who completed the questionnaire. You also calculated the mean scores for each group. They appeared different, but you could not really tell until an ANOVA procedure was applied to the data.

Step Three: You Set Up Your Data for Data Entry into a Database.

The data for your one-way ANOVA might be recorded in a database that looks like that shown in figure 8.1. There are three sets of parents with a total of 39 (N). The groups are not exactly the same size but are close enough not to seriously violate assumptions of equal group size. The parent group codes and the school support scores are listed. Only those two pieces of data are entered into your statistical formula or canned statistical package. This ensures confidentiality to those responding to the survey.

Step Four: You Execute the ANOVA Statistical Procedure to Obtain an F Ratio, the Calculated Value.

After you have entered your data from your database, you can execute the ANOVA. Whether you hand-calculate the ANOVA or use a "canned"

Parent	Category	Group Code	School Support Score
1. Mrs. Polinsky	Elementary	1	123
2. Ms. Morelli	Elementary	1	119
3. Mr. Anderson	Elementary	1	120
4. Ms. Delgado	Elementary	1	103
5. Ms. Adams	Elementary	1	168
6. Mr. Dinh	Elementary	1	190
7. Mrs. Lena	Elementary	1	120
8. Mrs. O'Brien	Elementary	1	130
9. Mr. Guzman	Elementary	1	103
10. Ms. Padilla	Elementary	1	104
11. Mr. Strada	Elementary	1	189
12. Ms. Hayes	Elementary	1	100
Group One	**N = 12**		**Mean = 130.75 (SD = 33)**
13. Ms. Kinane	Middle	2	120
14. Mr. Calafiore	Middle	2	190
15. Mrs. Dean	Middle	2	189
16. Ms. Chai	Middle	2	145
17. Ms. Quinn	Middle	2	171
18. Mr. Bentur	Middle	2	189
19. Ms. Chaduri	Middle	2	145
20. Mr. Chung	Middle	2	177
21. Ms. Bosco	Middle	2	189
22. Mr. Ross	Middle	2	167
23. Ms. Johnson	Middle	2	156
24. Ms. Piekos	Middle	2	189
Group Two	**N = 12**		**Mean = 168.92 (SD = 23)**
25. Mrs. Card	Secondary	3	120
26. Ms. Dombi	Secondary	3	134
27. Ms. Ryan	Secondary	3	155
28. Ms. Temkin	Secondary	3	134
29. Mr. Dickinson	Secondary	3	144
30. Ms. Crovo	Secondary	3	133
31. Mr. Rae	Secondary	3	142
32. Ms. Perez-Bohn	Secondary	3	123

Figure 8.1. Three groups of parents and school support scores for one-way ANOVA.

33. Mr. Amado	Secondary	3	110
34. Ms. Trinh	Secondary	3	102
35. Ms. Nulsen	Secondary	3	130
36. Ms. Schipul	Secondary	3	190
37. Ms. Trivella	Secondary	3	100
38. Ms. Rosenberg	Secondary	3	103
39. Ms. Reis	Secondary	3	120
Group Three	**N = 15**		**Mean = 129.33 (SD = 23)**

Figure 8.1.   Continued.

statistical package, the same result emerges: an F ratio. This is the statistic in ANOVA that indicates you can reject the null hypothesis.

Parallel to the *t*-test procedure, the F ratio is called the calculated value. It is usually a three- or four-digit number with two decimal places. The plus or minus sign does not matter; ignore it. For our data set, the calculated F ratio is 8.94.

Step Five: You Compare Your Calculated F Ratio to the Critical F Ratio in the F Distribution Table.

You have to compare your calculated F value to the critical F value, located at the end of many statistics textbooks. It is called the F distribution table. A portion of this is displayed in figure 8.2. For your data set, the calculated F ratio was 8.94. The critical value in the F distribution table was 3.26. You exceeded or beat the table value.

USING THE F DISTRIBUTION TABLE CORRECTLY: DEGREES OF FREEDOM

The degrees of freedom (*df*) for ANOVA procedures are a bit more complicated and can cause some confusion. There are two numbers that compose your degrees of freedom for ANOVA: the between-groups degrees of freedom and the within-groups degrees of freedom. The number for the *between-groups* degrees of freedom is equal to the number of groups minus one. In this case you had three parent groups. So the value for your between-groups degrees of freedom is 2. The value for the *within-groups* degrees of freedom is equal to the number in each group minus one and

Between →					$p < 0.5$					
Within ↓ DF	1	2	3	4	5	6	7	8	9	10
1	161	200	216	225	230	234	237	239	241	242
2	18.5	19.0	19.2	19.3	19.3	19.4	19.4	19.4	19.4	19.4
3	10.1	9.55	9.28	9.12	9.01	8.94	8.89	8.85	8.81	8.79
4	7.71	6.94	6.59	6.39	6.26	6.16	6.09	6.04	6.00	5.96
5	6.61	5.79	5.41	5.19	5.05	4.95	4.88	4.82	4.77	4.74
6	5.99	5.14	4.76	4.53	4.39	4.28	4.21	4.15	4.10	4.06
7	5.59	4.74	4.35	4.12	3.97	3.87	3.79	3.73	3.68	3.64
8	5.32	4.46	4.07	3.84	3.69	3.58	3.50	3.44	3.39	3.35
9	5.12	4.26	3.86	3.63	3.48	3.37	3.29	3.23	3.18	3.14
10	4.96	4.10	3.71	3.48	3.33	3.22	3.14	3.07	3.02	2.98
11	4.84	3.98	3.59	3.36	3.20	3.09	3.01	2.95	2.90	2.85
12	4.75	3.89	3.49	3.26	3.11	3.00	2.91	2.85	2.80	2.75
13	4.67	3.81	3.41	3.18	3.03	2.92	2.83	2.77	2.71	2.67
14	4.60	3.74	3.34	3.11	2.96	2.85	2.76	2.70	2.65	2.60
15	4.54	3.68	3.29	3.06	2.90	2.79	2.71	2.64	2.59	2.54
16	4.49	3.63	3.24	3.01	2.85	2.74	2.66	2.59	2.54	2.49
17	4.45	3.59	3.20	2.96	2.81	2.70	2.61	2.55	2.49	2.45
18	4.41	3.55	3.16	2.93	2.77	2.66	2.58	2.51	2.46	2.41
19	4.38	3.52	3.13	2.90	2.74	2.63	2.54	2.48	2.42	2.38
20	4.35	3.49	3.10	2.87	2.71	2.60	2.51	2.45	2.39	2.35
21	4.32	3.47	3.07	2.84	2.68	2.57	2.49	2.42	2.37	2.32
22	4.30	3.44	3.05	2.82	2.66	2.55	2.46	2.40	2.34	2.30
23	4.28	3.42	3.03	2.80	2.64	2.53	2.44	2.37	2.32	2.27
24	4.26	3.40	3.01	2.78	2.62	2.51	2.42	2.36	2.30	2.25
25	4.24	3.39	2.99	2.76	2.60	2.49	2.40	2.34	2.28	2.24
30	4.17	3.32	2.92	2.69	2.53	2.42	2.33	2.27	2.21	2.16
40	4.08	3.23	2.84	2.61	2.45	2.34	2.25	2.18	2.12	2.08
60	4.00	3.15	2.76	2.53	2.37	2.25	2.17	2.10	2.04	1.99
120	3.92	3.07	2.68	2.45	2.29	2.18	2.09	2.02	1.96	1.91
00	3.84	3.00	2.60	2.37	2.21	2.10	2.01	1.94	1.88	1.83

Figure 8.2. Partial F distribution table.

then the sum for each group. In your case the value for the within-groups degrees of freedom is 36. It is calculated like this.

Group 1 [12 – 1] + Group 2 [12 – 1] + Group 3 [15 – 1] or
11 + 11 + 14 = 36

The degrees of freedom numbers are 2 and 36. You will see the degrees of freedom often reported like this: (df = 2,36). To use the F distribution table correctly, you have to know that the value for the between-groups degrees of freedom is reported horizontally across the top of the table and that for the within-groups degrees of freedom is reported vertically down the side of the table. So, where these two numbers intersect in the table at your probability level of .05 or .01, there is your critical value. For df = 2,36, the critical table value is between 3.32 and 3.23 in the table.

Step Six: You Accept or Reject the Null Hypothesis.

Because your calculated value exceeds the critical value, you reject the null hypothesis.

There is a difference in levels of school support among elementary, middle, and secondary school parent leaders.

Step Seven: You Conduct Follow-up Tests to Your ANOVA.

When you have statistical differences with *t*-tests, there are only two mean scores. You can look to see which is higher and which is lower and then draw your conclusions and inferences. End of story. If you have a statistically significant result with ANOVA, your work is not complete. The only answer you have obtained at this point is that there are statistically significant differences among your groups—in this example, the three groups of parent leaders. But which groups are different on the variable of support? There are several possibilities where significant differences might exist.

- Between elementary and middle school parent leaders
- Between elementary and secondary school parent leaders

- Between secondary and middle school parent leaders
- Among all three different groups with each other

With ANOVA there are more than two mean scores. You cannot eyeball the scores and make deductions. You have to conduct an additional statistical procedure.

A follow-up test, called a *post hoc* procedure or multiple comparison test, is designed just for this purpose. It shows exactly where the significant differences lie after a significant F ratio is obtained in ANOVA. It pinpoints which mean scores are significantly different from each other.

There are many choices for *post hoc* procedures to choose from. Each is named after the scientist who developed it.

- Fisher's LSD test
- Duncan's new multiple range test
- Newman-Keuls test
- Tukey's HSD test
- Scheffé test

Some of these tests are more conservative than others are, making it harder to reject the null hypothesis. A liberal procedure will find a significant difference between two mean scores that are relatively close together. A conservative procedure will indicate that two mean scores are significantly different only when the means are far apart. From the previous list, the Fisher LSD is the most liberal and the Scheffé test the most conservative.

You may wonder why *t*-tests are not used to compare each of the combinations listed. That would be logical except for the fact that conducting multiple *t*-tests increases the chances of getting spurious results with error. As the number of *t*-tests increases, the probability of getting a statistically significant difference by chance alone increases. This means you are approaching Type I error territory! Multiple comparison tests adjust the level of significance to reduce the influence of chance results occurring.

For your sample you conduct a Scheffé multiple comparison test. It showed that at the $p < .05$ level your middle school parent leaders were significantly different from both the elementary and secondary school parent leaders on levels of school support. When we examine the three mean scores, we can see why. The middle school parent leaders have expressed a much higher level of support for your school, as documented by their mean score of 169 and smaller standard deviation of 23. As superintendent of schools, you have decided to recruit middle school parent leaders as the first cadre of image emissaries to spearhead your public relations campaign.

REPORTING ANOVA RESULTS IN A TABLE FORMAT

Figure 8.3 shows how you might report your findings in a table format for your report to the board of education.

There are other more sophisticated ways to report ANOVA findings. You can find them in professional journals in different formats. However, for a lay audience, this is all you need to tell them. It makes the point and establishes where the focus should be for action steps in following up decisions based on data.

Parent Groups	Mean	(SD)	F Ratio	df	p
Elementary School Parent group	131	(33)	8.94	2,36	.01**
Middle School Parent group	169	(23)			
Secondary School Parent group	129	(23)			

**$p < .01$

(Scheffé *post hoc:* Middle school group is significantly different from both elementary and secondary groups in levels of support. They have a higher level of support than either of the other two groups.)

Figure 8.3.   One-way ANOVA table.

OTHER VERSIONS OF ANOVA

There are other versions of ANOVA procedures besides one-way ANOVA. These become more complex because of the added variables in the research designs. If you are interested in using any of these, it may be wise to consult a professional with expertise in multivariate procedures. There are multiple F ratios, interaction effects, and other aspects that make the following procedures more sophisticated.

Factorial ANOVA

Factorial ANOVA designs compare *more* than one independent variable. Let's use the same example that we had in one-way ANOVA but add another independent variable, also referred to as a "factor." We subclassify the parent groups into the two hypothetical towns that represent your school system: town A and town B. So, now we have *parent group* as one independent variable and *town of residence* as a second independent variable. Instead of three groups that we had in one-way ANOVA, we have six groups because of the two independent variables. Each of the six groups' mean scores on your one dependent variable of *support* will be compared by the *two-way ANOVA* (see figure 8.4).

Elementary School Town A	Middle School Town A	Secondary School Town A
Elementary School Town B	Middle School Town B	Secondary School Town B

Figure 8.4.   Two-factor ANOVA: six parent groups.

This can further become a *three-way ANOVA* by adding yet another independent variable or third factor. Let's add "Voter status"—Registered /Not Registered. There are now three independent variables with 12 separate groups on which the dependent variable of level of support will be measured (see figure 8.5).

Elementary School Town A Registered to Vote	Middle School Town A Registered to Vote	Secondary School Town A Registered to Vote
Elementary School Town B Registered to Vote	Middle School Town B Registered to Vote	Secondary School Town B Registered to Vote
Elementary School Town A Not Registered to Vote	Middle School Town A Not Registered to Vote	Secondary School Town A Not Registered to Vote
Elementary School Town B Not Registered to Vote	Middle School Town B Not Registered to Vote	Secondary School Town B Not Registered to Vote

Figure 8.5.   Three-factor ANOVA: twelve parent groups.

ANCOVA

Another very useful statistical procedure is called *analysis of covariance* or *ANCOVA*. The purpose of this technique is to make groups equivalent before they are compared on the dependent variable.

As you may recall, one of the primary tenets of the *t*-test, as well as ANOVA procedures, is that the groups you are studying are alike *except* for your dependent variable. You want to ensure that something else (called extraneous variance or error) does not account for differences between or among the groups. The ANCOVA adjusts for differences so that the focus of the analysis is on the dependent variable and not tainted by error.

As an example, you, as a principal, are awarded a grant for an innovative program. It involves an instructional method thought to be effective in raising language arts skills. One of your teachers, Ms. Seymour, implements the new method with her classroom, while Mrs. Santo continues using the traditional instructional method in her classroom. When both classrooms are tested *before* the program begins, the results show statistically significant differences in language arts between the two classrooms; the mean scores are statistically different.

ANCOVA is used to statistically equate the two classrooms' scores on language arts skills before the innovative instructional method is implemented. This way the playing field is leveled, and we can have a baseline that is similar for both classrooms. This allows us to determine whether a real difference occurred over time. ANCOVA determines if the instructional methods produce different results in language arts skills, when the program is concluded, by equating the mean differences found at initial testing.

As a note, ANCOVA can be executed with two groups because the *t*-test does not have the capability to adjust for mean score differences. All ANOVA procedures, as mentioned earlier, can be done with two groups, if you wish, although most of the time a *t*-test better serves that purpose.

Repeated Measures ANOVA

There are occasions when we need to measure something on a recurrent basis. You measure the dependent variable more than once;

you repeatedly measure it. This is where the statistical procedure gets its name, *repeated-measures ANOVA*.

For example, you may have a group of students whose reading skills you want to track for changes. You test them in September, December, April, and again in June to determine their progress. Or you have a group of football players whose sprint times you measure before, during, and at the end of the football season. Or you measure the level of employee satisfaction with your school system in the current year and every year afterward to monitor the ebb and flow. All of these occasions might lend themselves to using a repeated-measures ANOVA procedure to determine changes over time and to track results.

CONCLUSION

The one-way ANOVA is a very useful statistic and a great partner to the *t*-test. It functions the same but affords us the opportunity to expand the number of groups beyond two. This is often called for in educational settings. The conceptual steps to ANOVA follow the *t*-test with the exception of the need to conduct *post hoc* tests after significant results are obtained. Many statistical packages offer this option as part of one-way ANOVA.

For statistical questions that are more complex (in that they add more dependent and independent variables to the research design), there are statistical models to accommodate them. Factorial ANOVA, ANCOVA, and repeated-measures ANOVAs are sophisticated statistical procedures that have been described in the most elementary fashion here. More detailed discussions are presented in statistical or mathematical textbooks. It may be wise to incorporate the assistance of someone with expertise in multivariate statistical analyses. In most educational settings, the statistics chosen for inclusion in this primer will be able to address most data for data-driven decisions.

9

TESTING YOUR HUNCH ABOUT DISTRIBUTIONS: CHI SQUARE ANALYSES

NONPARAMETRIC STATISTICS

In the last two chapters, we discussed parametric statistics that answer questions about differences between groups (*t*-tests) and among groups (ANOVAs). Although these parametric statistics are of great value and used often in educational settings, one of the most valuable statistics for educational leaders is a nonparametric procedure called chi square analysis. It is also called the test of "goodness of fit." Its symbol is "χ squared" (χ^2).

Compared to the *t*-test and ANOVA procedures, the chi square analysis is not as powerful to reject the null hypothesis. It does not use the mean or standard deviation for computation; it does not rely on an interval or ratio scaling. Because the chi square analysis relies on frequency data, its value lies in the statistic's ability to answer questions about data that are nominal. Variables in educational settings are measured very often by their categories—and not exact intervals. Chi square analysis allows you to answer important questions with variables measured with nominal or ordinal scales.

WALKING THROUGH THE STEPS FOR CONDUCTING A CHI SQUARE ANALYSIS

A rudimentary example of a chi square analysis will promote the merit of this statistical technique. Let's say that your secondary school was concerned about the shortfall of senior male students going on to four-year colleges. The graduating class of 80 students had 50% males (n = 40) and 50% females (n = 40) or 80 seniors in all.

Step One: You State Your Null Hypothesis.

There is no difference between male and female senior students on their postgraduation plans.

This null hypothesis sounds similar to the hypotheses for t-tests and ANOVAs, but there are no dependent and independent variables. Additionally, you can see that your two variables are nominally scaled. That is the essential magnificence of this statistical technique, the chi square.

Step Two: You Identify Your Two Categorical Variables.

The first is *gender* with two categories:

• Male
• Female

The second is *postgraduation plans* with four categories:

• Employment
• Two-year college
• Four-year college
• Technical college

Step Three: You Set Up a Contingency Table of Your Expected Frequencies.

A contingency table of expected frequencies is an arrangement of your categorical data into a two-way classification scheme. One of the classifications becomes *rows* (across), and the other becomes *columns* (down). The boxes, formed by the intersection of rows and columns, are called *cells*. The cells tell us what you can expect, given the frequencies of rows and columns. It is a simple application of probabilities based on your sample numbers and their classifications. Figure 9.1 displays a contingency table of expected frequencies for your data.

	Males	Females	Row Classification ↔
Employment	10 (25%)	10 (25%)	20 (25%)
Two-year college	10 (25%)	10 (25%)	20 (25%)
Four-year college	10 (25%)	10 (25%)	20 (25%)
Technical college	10 (25%)	10 (25%)	20 (25%)
Column Classification ↕	40 (50%)	40 (50%)	N = 80

Figure 9.1.   Contingency table of expected frequencies.

In the case of this example, the columns (down) correspond to gender with *two* categories. So you allocate two columns for each of the two gender categories. The rows (across) correspond to the variable of postgraduation plans and have *four* different categories. You allocate four rows for each of the four postgraduation plans. You have 80 students altogether.

The classification for "columns" creates two categories of gender. Half of the students are males (40, or 50%) and half are females (40, or 50%). The "rows" for postgraduation plans break into four categories and are employment (20, or 25%), two-year college (20, or 25%), four-year college (20, or 25%), and technical college (20, or 25%).

Then you have to calculate the cells. The expected frequency of any cell in the table is found by multiplying the total of the column with the total of the row to which the cell belongs. The product is divided by the total sample size. So to obtain a cell for males, you multiply the total of the column (40) times the total of the row (20) and divide by 80, the sample size. You get 10 as your cell size. This is your expected frequency for each cell. It is helpful to report the cell size as well as its percentage. The table for expected frequencies has both.

You have just constructed a table of expected frequencies from the two nominal variables for your 80 students. Each cell has 10 students in it because of the breakdown of the two classification variables: gender and postgraduation. So what you would *expect* for your seniors as outcomes is that 10 females and 10 males will pursue each of the four postgraduation plans.

When to Collapse Categories to Make Cells Larger   The table enables you to determine the nature of the relationships between your two categorical variables. As a recommendation, you should have at least five values in each cell. If not, it might be a good idea to collapse or combine a category in one of your variables to make the cell larger. This is important for statistical analysis with the chi square approach. As an example, the categorical variable of marital status might reveal that the category of "widowed" has only three members. You may want to combine it with the category of "single" to increase the size of data points in the category.

Step Four: You Set Up Your Data for Data Entry into a Database.

Figure 9.2 shows the list that you have been given. It indicates the postgraduation plans for your 80 seniors.

ID	Males	Post Graduation		ID	Females	Post Graduation
1.	Robert	Employment		1.	Rita	2 yr. college
2.	Peter	2 yr. college		2.	Susan	4 yr. college
3.	Bill	Tech college		3.	Brenda	2 yr. college
4.	Angel	2 yr. collge		4.	Maura	4 yr. college
5.	Jose	Employment		5.	Felice	2 yr. college
6.	Mike	Tech college		6.	Allison	4 yr. college
7.	David	Tech college		7.	Amelia	4 yr. college
8.	Seth	Employment		8.	Ellen	4 yr. college
9.	Charles	2 yr. college		9.	Emily	4 yr. college
10.	TJ	Tech college		10.	Alyssa	4 yr. college
11.	Frank	2 yr. college		11.	Krista	2 yr. college
12.	Guy	Employment		12.	Kara	4 yr. college
13.	Paul	Tech college		13.	Annie	Employment
14.	Al	2 yr. college		14.	Julia	Employment
15.	Jack	Employment		15.	Olivia	2 yr. college
16.	Barry	Tech college		16.	Joanne	Employment
17.	Tommy	Employment		17.	Mary Grace	4 yr. college
18.	Eddie	Tech college		18.	Jennie	4 yr. college
19.	Peter	Tech college		19.	Yolanda	2 yr. college
20.	Tony	2 yr. college		20.	Michelle	4 yr. college
21.	John	Tech college		21.	Estelle	Employment

Figure 9.2.   Data set for seniors by gender and postgraduation plans.

22.	Matt	Employment		22.	Cheryl	4 yr. college
23.	Roger	2 yr. college		23.	Gail	4 yr. college
24.	Jeff	Tech college		24.	Robin	4 yr. college
25.	Owen	Employment		25.	Martha	2 yr. college
26.	James	2 yr. college		26.	Janice	Employment
27.	Miquel	Tech college		27.	Judy	4 yr. college
28.	Bobby	Employment		28.	Katherine	2 yr. college
29.	Jim	Tech college		29.	Polly	4 yr. college
30.	Terry	Employment		30.	Charla	Employment
31.	Timmy	Tech college		31.	Jewel	2 yr. college
32.	Denzel	2 yr. college		32.	Avital	4 yr. college
33.	Drake	Tech college		33.	Leora	4 yr. college
34.	Albert	Tech college		34.	Margie	Employment
35.	Joe	2 yr. college		35.	Jeanne	4 yr. college
36.	Mark	Tech college		36.	Cindy	2 yr. college
37.	Daniel	Tech college		37.	Linda	Employment
38.	Jesus	Tech college		38.	Lois	4 yr. college
39.	Ray	Tech college		39.	Amy	Employment
40.	Zack	Tech college		40.	Lucy	Employment

Figure 9.2.   Continued.

You have decided to code gender as:

- Male (1)
- Female (2)

The postgraduation plan has been coded:

- Employment (1)
- Two-year college (2)
- Four-year college (3)
- Technical college (4)

The data set is scrambled. You decide to organize the data set, dividing it into two separate groups: males and females. Then, you use the "sort" command in your word processing package to sort on the variable of postgraduation plan by gender. Figure 9.3 shows what the data now look like. The data are much more manageable. You can easily count the categories and their respective frequencies. This is a great time-saver. For data entry, you will only use numeric data, as figure 9.3 reflects.

ID #	Gender	Post Grad	ID #	Gender	Post Grad
1.	1	2	41.	2	2
2.	1	2	42.	2	2
3.	1	2	43.	2	2
4.	1	2	44.	2	2
5.	1	2	45.	2	2
6.	1	2	46.	2	2
7.	1	2	47.	2	2
8.	1	2	48.	2	2
9.	1	2	49.	2	2
10.	1	2	50.	2	2
11.	1	1	51.	2	3
12.	1	1	52.	2	3
13.	1	1	53.	2	3
14.	1	1	54.	2	3
15.	1	1	55.	2	3
16.	1	1	56.	2	3
17.	1	1	57.	2	3
18.	1	1	58.	2	3
19.	1	1	59.	2	3
20.	1	1	60.	2	3
21.	1	4	61.	2	3
22.	1	4	62.	2	3
23.	1	4	63.	2	3
24.	1	4	64.	2	3
25.	1	4	65.	2	3
26.	1	4	66.	2	3
27.	1	4	67.	2	3
28.	1	4	68.	2	3
29.	1	4	69.	2	3
30.	1	4	70.	2	3
31.	1	4	71.	2	1
32.	1	4	72.	2	1
33.	1	4	73.	2	1

Figure 9.3.   Data set for seniors, gender, and postgraduation plans.

34.	I	4	74.	2	I
35.	I	4	75.	2	I
36.	I	4	76.	2	I
37.	I	4	77.	2	I
38.	I	4	78.	2	I
39.	I	4	79.	2	I
40.	I	4	80.	2	I

Figure 9.3. Continued.

Step Five: You Set Up a Contingency Table of Your Actual Frequencies.

You are going to set up a table with your actual outcome data. The actual frequency data from your senior class creates the contingency table of actual frequencies. You look at your first contingency table of *expected* frequencies and then review the contingency table of *actual* frequencies. The cells appear to be statistically different, but you subject your data to statistical analysis—in this case a chi square analysis. It is an exceptional statistic to determine if postgraduation plans for male and females seniors are in fact different (see figure 9.4).

Step Six: You Execute the Chi Square Statistical Procedure to Obtain a Calculated Value.

After you have entered your data from your database into the statistical program of your choice, you execute the chi square procedure. You can also hand-calculate the statistic by using a formula found in any

	Males	Females	Row Classification ↔
Employment	10 (25%)	10 (25%)	20 (25%)
Two-year college	10 (25%)	10 (25%)	20 (25%)
Four-year college	0 (0%)	20 (50%)	20 (25%)
Technical college	20 (50%)	0 (0%)	20 (25%)
Column Classification ↕	40 (50%)	40 (50%)	N = 80

Figure 9.4. Contingency table of actual frequencies.

statistics or mathematics textbook. Either way, after you execute the chi square statistical procedure, you obtain a chi square of 40.00. This is called your *calculated value*.

Step Seven: You Compare Your Calculated Chi Square Value to the Critical Chi Square Value.

Next, you compare your calculated value to what is called the critical value located in a statistical table, called the chi square distribution table. It is displayed in figure 9.5.

df	Chi Square P < .05	Chi Square P < .01
1	3.84	6.64
2	5.99	9.21
3	7.82	11.34
4	9.49	13.28
5	11.07	15.09
6	12.59	16.81
7	14.07	15.09
8	15.51	20.09
9	16.92	21.67
10	18.31	23.21
11	19.68	24.72
12	21.03	26.22
13	22.36	27.69
14	23.68	39.14
15	25.00	30.58
16	26.30	32.00
17	27.59	33.41
18	28.87	34.80
19	30.14	36.19
20	31.41	37.57
21	32.67	38.93
22	33.92	40.29

Figure 9.5.   Partial chi square distribution table.

23	35.17	41.64
24	36.42	42.98
25	37.65	44.31
26	38.88	45.64
27	40.11	46.96
28	41.34	48.28
29	42.56	49.59
30	43.77	50.89

Figure 9.5.   Continued.

Degrees of Freedom   The value for degrees of freedom (*df*) for a chi square statistic is calculated by taking (the number of rows − 1) × (the number of columns − 1). In the case of your seniors, you have two rows (gender categories) and four columns (postgraduation plans). So the value for degrees of freedom equals (2 − 1) × (4 − 1) or 3.

$$[2 - 1] = 1 \times [4 - 1] = 3 \text{ or } 1 \times 3 = 3 \text{ degrees of freedom}$$

If your calculated value exceeds the critical value in the statistical table, you reject the null hypothesis. If not, you accept the null hypothesis as true.

Step Eight: You Accept or Reject the Null Hypothesis.

For 3 degrees of freedom at the .05 level of probability, the critical chi square table value is actually 7.82. It is shaded in figure 9.5 so that you can see how it was located in the table. Because your calculated value for the chi square is 40.00, you exceeded the table value. The expected frequencies were significantly different from what you observed to be true in your actual data. So you reject the null hypothesis.

There is a difference between male and female seniors on postgraduation plans.

REPORTING CHI SQUARE RESULTS IN A TABLE FORMAT

From the study of seniors and postgraduation outcomes, you want to present the findings to the board of education and parent-teachers association

Seniors N = 80	Frequencies/ Outcomes	Employment	Two-year College	Four-year College	Technical College	χ2
Males	Expected	10 (25%)	10 (25%)	10 (25%)	10 (25%)	40.00*
40 = n	Actual	10 (25%)	10 (25%)	0 (0%)	20 (50%)	
Females	Expected	10 (25%)	10 (25%)	10 (25%)	10 (25%)	
40 = n	Actual	10 (25%)	10 (25%)	20 (50%)	0 (0%)	

*P < .05

Figure 9.6.   Reporting the chi square results in table format.

in your secondary school. Figure 9.6 shows a simple format for reporting chi square results. There are more sophisticated ways to report chi square findings. You can locate them in professional journals. However, for a lay audience, this is all you need to say. It makes the point and establishes where the focus should be for action steps in following up decisions based on data.

CONCLUSION

The chi square statistic, which relies on nominal scaling described in chapter 1, is used heavily in educational environments. The chi square statistical procedure allows us to compare groups with each other on important variables. Although it may not have the sophistication of its parametric counterparts, its utility may exceed theirs. It is a statistical technique that provides us with insights about students, schools, and stakeholders that would be impossible to diagnose if you had to depend on statistics that required interval or ratio scaling.

(10)

TESTING YOUR HUNCH ABOUT
RELATIONSHIPS: CORRELATION

In addition to focusing on differences, data-driven decisions are often focused on relationships. There are many times in educational settings when we wonder if two factors are linked. For example, we may ask some of the following questions:

- Does the degree of summer tutoring increase standardized test scores?
- Does taking Ritalin reduce student behavioral problems in the classroom?
- Does the level of teacher satisfaction reduce turnover?
- Does enrollment in advanced placement courses increase student acceptance at selective colleges?
- Does the extent of community involvement assist in passing school referenda?

There are statistics that help to determine if relationships do exist, and, if so, what the characteristics of those relationships are. This is where correlations are useful statistical techniques. They test the extent to which two variables occur together and how related they are. As statistics, correlations can be descriptive and inferential at the same time.

They can describe your data, and you can also infer relationships from samples to populations.

WHAT DATA YOU NEED TO PRODUCE CORRELATIONS

You need two sets of variables (or paired observations) on the same individuals. In correlations, the first variable is called x. The second variable is called y. Your data are paired observations of x and y on one person. You correlate x and y to see if there is a relationship. For the purpose of illustration, let's say that we wanted to know if height and weight were related for kindergarten children entering our school. We thought if you were taller, you would weigh more. If you were shorter, you would weigh less. Height and weight would be our two variables for our paired observations. We would collect our data on all kindergarten children. For each child in kindergarten, we would have weight (x) and height (y). Then we would calculate a correlation statistic and find the answer.

There are basically four conceptual areas that correlational procedures address. Each is followed by an example of variables that you might correlate with each other.

1. If one variable [x] *increases,* does the other variable [y] *increase?*
   Example: More study time increases test performance.
2. If one variable [x] *decreases,* does the other variable [y] *decrease?*
   Example: Poor school attitude reduces positive in-school behavior.
3. If one variable [x] *increases,* does the other variable [y] *decrease?*
   Example: Increased salary and benefits reduce staff turnover.
4. If one variable [x] *decreases,* does the other variable [y] *increase?*
   Example: Low parental support increases the incidence of school absences.

CORRELATION COEFFICIENTS

The relationship between two variables, and the nature of that relationship, are measured by *a correlation coefficient,* symbolized by the letter *r*. A correlation coefficient is a two-digit decimal such as –.20 or +.78. The numerical values can range from –1.00 through zero to +1.00. However, –1.00 and +1.00 are perfect correlations and you hardly ever see these numbers in the real world. There is a formula for calculating a correlation coefficient; it is found in any statistical text. There are several versions, however. The different types are based on the scales used in measuring your variables; they will be discussed shortly.

The correlation coefficient is an amazing statistic because a single number summarizes the *strength* and the *direction* of the relationship between two variables.

STRENGTH

The *actual numeric value* of the correlation coefficient tells us the strength of the relationship. The nearer the number is to either +1.00 or –1.00, the stronger the relationship is between the two variables. Correlations of –.88 and +.88 have the same strength. A correlation of –.88 is stronger than a correlation of +.87 by only an infinitesimal amount.

A zero correlation (*r* = 0) indicates absolutely no correlation whatsoever. The relationship between class size and teacher's salary would have no correlation (*r* = 0). Correlations of –.07 or +.02 are negligible. Although there is no hard and firm interpretation of what constitutes strength, here are some correlation coefficients with interpretation of strength suggested.

Correlation Coefficient	Strength
0	No correlation
±.01 to ±.30	Negligible to low
±.31 to ±.50	Moderately low
±.51 to ±.70	Moderate
±.71 to ±.99	Very strong
±1.00	Perfect

CORRELATIONS AND SHARED VARIANCE

As a note, a correlation coefficient should not be interpreted as a percentage. Because it is a decimal, this can happen but is incorrect. If the correlation between teacher salary and level of teacher turnover is .50 (r), you cannot conclude that teacher salary accounts for 50% of teacher turnover. You must square the correlation coefficient and multiply it by 100 to assess the shared variance of two variables. This is called a *coefficient of determination* (noted by r^2). For this example, 25% (r^2) is the shared variance between the two variables of teacher salary and turnover. You can conclude that 25% of turnover can be explained by salary. This coefficient of determination (r^2) is the percentage of variance held in common by the two variables. The following chart indicates the correlation coefficients and the percentage of shared variance. As you can see, you must have an extremely high correlation to assume that two variables are part of each other.

Correlation (r)	Coefficient of Determination (r^2)
.10	1%
.15	2%
.25	6%
.50	25%
.75	56%
.80	64%
.90	81%
.95	90%
.98	96%

DIRECTION

Relationships between two variables can be either positive or negative. That is what is meant by "direction." Therefore, correlation coefficients can be either positive or negative. A plus or a minus sign before the numeric value indicates direction.

If a correlation is positive, it means that

- If one variable (x) increases, the other (y) increases, *or*
- If one variable decreases (x), the other (y) decreases.

Positive correlations sometimes have a plus sign before the decimal, but often it is implied. So a positive correlation of +.67 might also look like .67. *If a correlation is negative*, it means that

- If one variable (x) increases, the other (y) decreases, or
- If one variable (x) decreases the other (y) increases.

There is always a minus sign before the correlation to indicate a negative correlation. These are also called *inverse* correlations.

WALKING THROUGH THE STEPS FOR CONDUCTING A CORRELATION STATISTICAL TECHNIQUE

The following example will demonstrate the qualities of asking questions with correlational statistics. Let's say that you have 20 students in your seventh grade. As the principal, you believe that students who participate in after-school clubs and extracurricular activities have better attendance in school. You want to show that this is true because it can serve as powerful information for decision making in your school with the board of education, with your professional staff, and with parents.

Step One: You State Your Null Hypothesis.

There is no relationship between participation in after-school/ extracurricular activities and school attendance.

Step Two: You Identify Your Two Variables: x and y.

Your variable x is the total number of school days in attendance, as tabulated at the end of the school year. The variable y is the total number of after-school and extracurricular activities the child participated in during the school year.

Step Three: You Set Up Your Data for Data Entry into a Database.

See figure 10.1.

Students	Attendance Out of 180 Possible Days	Number of Extracurricular Activities
	x	y
1. Alex	140	1
2. Jason	170	7
3. Allison	150	2
4. Amelia	135	2
5. Thea	160	5
6. Carrie	175	8
7. Ellen	160	6
8. Emily	155	3
9. Felice	165	8
10. Juan	135	2
11. Julia	180	8
12. Krista	165	7
13. Kara	145	3
14. Mark	140	3
15. Miguel	155	3
16. Mike	145	1
17. Olivia	175	8
18. Rachael	180	7
19. Rebecca	170	7
20. Seth	175	9

Figure 10.1. Data set for attendance and extracurricular activities.

Step Four: You Set Up a Scattergram.

Before you run your correlational procedure, you set up a graph of your data. As we learned with frequency distributions, graphing techniques can be very informative in illustrating a message quickly and succinctly. Similar to a frequency polygon, the scattergram is a graphic representation of your correlation data.

You start again with the vertical (ordinate) and horizontal (abscissa) axes on a graph. For your data set, you place the "number of club or ex-

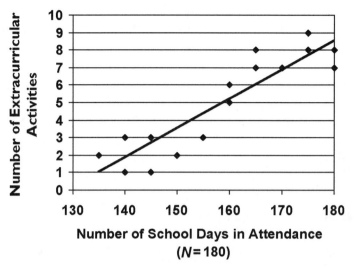

Figure 10.2.   Scattergram: positive correlation.

tracurricular activities" on the vertical axis starting with 1 and ending with 10, a little above the highest value in your data set.

On the horizontal axis are the total days in attendance in the school year. Then, you plot variables x and y for each child on your graph. Place a dot on the graph where the two variables intersect. Our scattergram looks like figure 10.2.

What Scattergrams Can Tell Us   Scattergrams are very useful because they tell a lot about our two variables and their relationship. Here are the pieces of information that scattergrams supply:

1. Scattergrams can *tell us the strength* of the relationship between the two variables.

   - If the dots cluster close to an imaginary line, there is a very strong relationship or correlation between the two variables.
   - When the dots are scattered in an ellipse or cigar shape, there is a moderate correlation.
   - When the dots are scattered randomly around the graph, there is a low or negligible correlation.

   The dots are clustering close to an imaginary line (the line penciled in on the scatter diagram in figure 10.2). We think that there might be a very strong relationship between the two variables. We have to execute a correlation statistic to truly find out, but the signs are there that a strong relationship exists.

Dots on the scattergram have another important function. Sometimes they are reviewed to determine the degree that one variable can predict the other. The more that the dots form that imaginary line or cigar-shape in an ellipse, the stronger the prediction. In this case, the diagonal line through the spread of dots is called the "regression line" or the "line of best fit." The tighter the clustering of dots, the better one variable is at predicting another. In the case of our data set, the number of extracurricular activities might be considered a predictor of school attendance. The dots are clustered into a fairly tight line.

2. Scattergrams can tell us the direction of the relationship between the two variables.

- If the slope of the line falls from left to right, there is a negative correlation.
- If the slope of the line rises from left to right, there is a positive correlation.

The latter is the case with the data in our scattergram. The slope of the line rises from left to right, signifying a positive correlation. The slope of the line indicates that as clubs and extracurricular activities increase, so does school attendance. Conversely, a positive relationship *also* means that as clubs and extracurricular activities decrease, so does attendance. Just looking at the slope tells us a great deal about the relationship between these two variables.

3. Scattergrams can also show outliers or oddball scores. Observations completely out of range with all the others should be considered for elimination in the calculation of a correlation coefficient. They might contaminate the data set and give misleading results if a correlation coefficient is calculated. In our example, there are no outlier scores. All of our x-y intersections fall close to the line.

Figure 10.3 shows several scattergrams and the messages they convey.

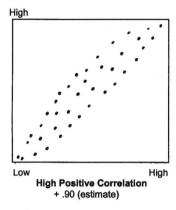

High Positive Correlation
+ .90 (estimate)

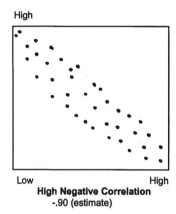

High Negative Correlation
-.90 (estimate)

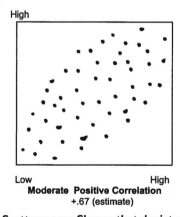

Moderate Positive Correlation
+.67 (estimate)

Figure 10.3. Scattergrams: Shapes that depict correlations.

Step Five: You Execute the Correct
Correlation Statistical Procedure.

You have looked at the scattergram and have a sense that a strong positive correlation exists between extracurricular activities and school attendance. Now, you want the statistical proof. You need to execute the proper correlation technique because there are many. The correct one should be selected carefully by characteristics in your data. The types of measurement scales for your two variables determine the type of correlation coefficient you use. This is where the awareness of scales, discussed in chapter 1, is so critical.

Types of Correlation Techniques for Correlating Two Variables

- *Pearson product moment correlation* is a parametric statistic and requires interval or ratio data on both the x and the y variables to calculate it. This is the premier correlation statistic. As a parametric statistic, the assumptions of homogeneity of variance and normal distribution apply, just as they do with t-test and ANOVAs. Pearson product moment correlation is called Pearson r. We will be using this for our example because our data meet the measurement scale requirements.
- *Point biserial procedure* is a nonparametric statistic and uses a dichotomous, nominal-scaled variable and an interval/ratio-scaled variable to calculate it. An example might be correlating the use of Ritalin (yes/no) *and* frequency of behavioral problems in the classroom.
- *Spearman rho* is a nonparametric statistic that uses ordinal-scaled data with ordinal-scaled data for computation. It correlates two sets of ranks to determine their degree of equivalence. An example might be the relationship between students' satisfaction levels *and* their agreement with school policy on smoking on school grounds.
- *Rank biserial* is a nonparametric statistic and uses a dichotomous, nominal-scaled variable and an ordinal-scaled variable to calculate it. An example is language spoken in the home (Spanish/English) *and* satisfaction with communication from school to the home.
- *Phi coefficient* is a nonparametric statistic and correlates two dichotomous, nominal-scaled variables. An example might be the re-

lationship between gender (boys and girls) *and* participation in the athletics program (yes/no).

For our example, we used a Pearson product moment correlation co-efficient and obtained a correlation coefficient of $r = +.78$. This is our *calculated* value. From the plus sign and from the size of the correlation coefficient we can immediately tell that we have a strong positive corre-lation.

Step Six: You Compare Your Calculated *r* Value to the Critical *r* Value.

Next, you compare your calculated value to the critical value located in a correlation statistical table usually found at the end of any research or statistics book. The value for the degrees of freedom (*df*) for a Pearson product moment correlation statistic is the number of pairs minus 2. In this case you have 20 pairs of data on students, so your value for *df* is (20 pairs − 2) or 18. Using figure 10.4, you compare your correlation coeffi-cient of .78 to the table value that is .44 at the $p < .05$ level and find that you have a significant relationship between after-school/extracurricular activities and school attendance. The correlation table is displayed with the critical value in boldface to show how it is located in the table.

Step Seven: You Accept or Reject the Null Hypothesis.

Because your calculated correlation coefficient is .78, you exceeded the table value and can reject the null hypothesis:

There is a relationship between after-school/extracurricular activities and school attendance.

Furthermore, the direction and strength tell you that as one increases so does the other. Participation in these activities boosts school atten-dance. Now, you have to determine as an educational leader how to get more students involved in these activities in the future. You bring the in-formation to the board of education, your professional staff, and your parents for their help and ideas.

df	r P < .05	P < .01	df	r P < .05	P < .01
1	.997	1.000	24	.388	.496
2	.950	.990	25	.381	.487
3	.878	.959	26	.374	.478
4	.811	.917	27	.367	.470
5	.754	.874	28	.361	.463
6	.707	.834	29	.355	.456
7	.666	.798	30	.349	.449
8	.632	.765	35	.325	.418
9	.602	.735	40	.304	.393
10	.602	.735	40	.304	.393
11	.553	.684	50	.273	.354
12	.532	.661	60	.250	.325
13	.514	.641	70	.232	.302
14	.497	.623	80	.217	.283
15	.482	.606	90	.205	.267
16	.468	.590	100	.195	.254
17	.456	.575	125	.174	.228
18	.444	.561	150	.159	.208
19	.433	.549	200	.138	.181
20	.423	.537	300	.113	.148
21	.413	.526	400	.098	.128
22	.404	.515	500	.088	.115
23	.396	.505	1000	.062	.081

Figure 10.4.   Correlation coefficient table.

SAMPLE SIZE AND SIGNIFICANCE OF CORRELATION COEFFICIENTS

As a note, the likelihood of obtaining a statistically significant correlation coefficient is based on sample size. If you have a large sample,
you often have a significant correlation coefficient. For example, you

can have 92 pairs of data and at the .05 level of statistical significance (df = 90) a correlation of r = .21 would be statistically significant, as you can see if you find this in the table in figure 10.4. This is a low correlation! However, the strength of the correlation coefficient is much more important for data-driven decisions. Smart educational leaders will know this very important fact. Those who are less informed would use statistical significance to make their case, and it would be a deceiving one due to sample size alone. If there is an investment of time or dollars that hinges on the correlation, look at the strength of the correlation coefficient and pay much less attention to whether it is statistically significant.

REPORTING CORRELATION RESULTS

Reporting a correlation coefficient is very simple. Just use r and the equal sign. For example, for our data set we would report that there was a strong correlation between after-school, extracurricular activities and school attendance (r = .78). That is it. You may want to show your actual data set. The scattergram for illustration would highlight the impact that one variable had on the other.

PRACTICAL APPLICATION OF CORRELATIONS

Educational leaders can use correlations in many ways.

1. The most useful purpose is to see if two variables are correlated. This is what chapter 10 has focused on.
2. Another important function of the correlation procedure is with respect to tests or instruments we measure with. The reliability of a test is reported as a correlation coefficient. It measures whether the test *consistently* measures what it is intended to measure. You can be confident of that when you examine the correlation coefficient, reported in the test manual as the "reliability coefficient." If it is r = .80 or r = .75, we can be certain that it is a pretty reliable

measurement tool. IQ tests have high reliability coefficients; personality tests or vocational interest assessments would have lower reliability coefficients.

3. A third function is performed by correlational statistics. If you are interested in determining whether two raters or two observers are seeing the same thing when they collect information, you are looking for inter-rater reliability. For example, if two of your teachers were evaluating the amount of time on task for the same group of students, you would want their observations (maybe recorded by a checklist) to be very similar. By correlating their data, you would create a reliability coefficient. It is hoped that the numeric value would be strong. This, too, is a use of correlation coefficients.

Correlating More Than Two Variables

The possibility of correlating more than two variables is ever present in the educational setting. However, this is where more complex statistical expertise is required. There are assumptions that must be adhered to in order to produce reliable and valid findings on which decisions will be based.

When you correlate more than two variables you are undertaking a multivariate statistical analysis called multiple correlation or multiple regression. This technique can be used for prediction purposes and has been frequently used to predict college freshmen grade-point averages (GPA) with both forms of the SAT (math and verbal) and high school Rank in Class (RIC). The formula below shows the prediction equation with the three predictors (x^1, x^2, and x^3) and what is predicted ($\hat{Y}$).

$$x^1(\text{RIC}) + x^2\,(\text{SATm}) + x^3\,(\text{SATv}) + \text{constant (a)} = \text{GPA}\,(\hat{Y}).$$

There are two conditions that should exist when you use this multivariate technique.

1. The variables that you are using to predict with should have a low correlation with each other. In this case, high school GPA, SATv, and SATm should have low inter-correlations. They are called the predictors.

2. The predictor variables, however, should have a high correlation with the variable that they are trying to predict—in this case college GPA. This is called the criterion variable.

Please refer to other statistics books for in-depth discussion of multiple regression and other multivariate procedures.

CONCLUSION

There is one last and very important point to make when correlations are discussed. No attempt should be made to say that one variable (x) causes the other variable (y). This is untrue. A correlation only suggests that a relationship exists. It does not mean that one causes the other. The correlational statistic is a great asset in educational settings. It can be used to show that relationships exists. To use a correlational statistic to pinpoint causality is a misuse of an unpretentious but highly valuable statistical tool.

11

TELLING YOUR STORY: REPORTING RESULTS

There is an inherent difficulty in getting people to read reports. Regardless of the relevance of the findings to the intended audience, the presence of a research-based methodology and the inclusion of statistics in a document are a turnoff for most readers. Attention must be paid both to how the report looks and to how it delivers its points. This is particularly true if the report is directed at lay readers such as members of the board of education, parents, and community members. Most are not educators. Reports should be developed in the mindset of the lay community of stakeholders.

Listed below are tips for formatting reports and presenting results that will make it easier for readers to understand and to evaluate the information in your report. All of these points should be considered in advance of tackling the job of compiling a report. If you think out a plan in advance, it will eliminate a lot of stress when you are knee deep in words and numbers.

Tip One: Use a Standard Organizational Framework to Format the Report.

The report is the official record of your research process. The organization is important for telling your story (the results or findings) and for keeping readers connected to it. The reader needs to follow a logical sequence to understand the purpose of the study, why certain decisions were made, and how findings were arrived at. A well-constructed report will provide the reader with all of the necessary information regarding the reasons for the research and the questions to be answered, the scope of the research, the design strategy and the sampling procedures, the methods of data collection and the instruments, the groups involved, the findings, and the summary comments and recommendations. This is the skeleton of any good story: a beginning, a middle, and an ending. A report of your study should have the methodology in the beginning, what you found out in the middle, and what the results mean at the end. This is a logical thought process that any reader can accept.

Tip Two: Keep the Text Concise and to the Point.

Most people reading your report do not want to spend a lot of time doing so. They want to get a handle on the findings and recommendations and then get on with their lives. Some report writers tend to repeat themselves, making the same point over and over. Some bury a main finding in so much verbiage that the reader becomes confused or misses it entirely. Sometimes two points are grouped together, also adding to confusion. If the point is worth making, the reader will pick up on it. As simple as it sounds, make your points one at a time. Keep the text simple, clear, and readable, without run-on sentences and extraneous descriptive language. High-sounding language is not impressive and will only diminish the impact of your findings.

Use short sentences and simple points. Make the report straightforward. Boil it down, and then boil it down again. If the tables are well conceived, a lot of narrative is unnecessary. Do not add educational or statistical jargon that the reader is unfamiliar with. If it is absolutely essential, make it user-friendly by defining it and its purpose. Otherwise, leave it out. This is neither a doctoral dissertation nor an academic journal article. It is a road map for action to benefit your school system.

Tip Three: Select a Typestyle That Is Easy to Read.

Typestyles should facilitate the ease with which the reader is able to scan the page. This point sounds simple and is perhaps considered an unnecessary one to make. However, it is important that the report be viewed as inviting and easy on the eye. A difficult typestyle can detract from the content of the report. A report written entirely in italics will not be fully digested, whereas those in Times New Roman, Comic Sans MS, and Arial will likely be read.

Tip Four: Use Boldface, Italics, and Uppercase with Deliberation.

There should be a reason why you shift from regular typeface to boldface, italics, and capitalization. A method to the madness should be evident. You may be making a point that needs special emphasis. You may be introducing a new concept or key word. You may be establishing an important heading for change in narrative discussion. Whatever the reason, have one before you add these embellishments. If the reader does not immediately see the rationale, he or she may skip parts of the text.

Tip Five: Use Tables to Present and Illustrate Your Findings.

Tables can be your best friend in writing the main body of the report—the findings. Usually, the tables are developed after the statistics are tabulated. This means that you have the tables to use when you tackle the narrative portion. Writing directly from the tables, generated by the study, will take the guesswork out of organizing the findings. It will be easy to present the findings logically in a way the reader can follow. Tables visually present a considerable amount of information to the reader in a way that can be readily understood. They allow the writer the opportunity to use a minimum amount of text to make key points.

Tip Six: Keep the Tables Simple.

Some tables are intimidating because of the large amounts of numbers they present to the reader. There is no way that most lay audience members can (or even want to) figure out what these types of tables represent. It is recommended that only one or two variables be presented in one table for a lay reader. This enables the reader to see your point, not be confused, and assimilate the message or finding. If you are reporting gender and grade levels, that is enough in one table. Instead of putting several variables in one table, use several tables to simplify the presentation. Keep that hat of the lay reader on your head.

Tip Seven: Do Not Report Numbers without Percentages.

In your tables that describe categorical variables or those variables with nominal or ordinal scales, do not list the numbers in each category without the corresponding percentages. With raw numbers only, you make the reader work too hard. Again, make the data easy for readers to grasp. Percentages convert raw data into meaningful information. The message is immediate and clear.

Tip Eight: Consider Including Graphs If They Add to Comprehension of the Findings.

The prudent use of frequency polygons, histograms, bar charts, pictographs, pie charts, and scattergrams is strongly urged. If they add to the story you are telling, put them in the report. If not, leave them out. Above all, use them if there is an inherent message that is conveyed. Do not add "so what" graphs; it wastes the reader's time. Sometimes the sizzle of our computer capabilities overrides our judgment in the use of visuals. In a report of written findings, they have less of a role. Their premier showcase is using them to make a visual PowerPoint presentation to an audience when the report is orally presented.

Tip Nine: Interpret Findings.

One of the greatest challenges (but one that true leaders embrace) is interpretation of findings. What does this all mean? Do not assume that readers will be able to infer the practical implications of what you are reporting. Tell them. This will avoid confusion, frustration, and most of all misinterpretation of the results. Furthermore, tell readers what action steps you believe are appropriate, given the results. You do not need to call them "recommendations" if you believe that word is heavy-handed. You can simply list your suggestions. However, laypersons look to you for that insight. You are the expert in the educational arena. Even a few action steps, suggestions, or recommendations will give the report added weight and value.

Tip Ten: Add an Executive Summary of Findings.

If you have an exceptionally long report, it is likely that it will not be read by everyone (as tough as that realization is on our ego). So you want to provide a summary of your salient points. What do you want readers to remember? This is what constitutes an executive summary. As the report does, the executive summary should have a beginning, a middle, and an ending. It should be broken down into sections with the use of bullets, boldfacing, or italics. The style should be readable, simple, and straightforward, as the whole report is. Encourage the reader to refer to the entire report if he or she needs to know more. Finally, this is the written document that will be disseminated and shared with the public, the media, and many others. It needs to be carefully written so that it summarizes your findings thoroughly, honestly, and succinctly.

Tip Eleven: Add a Glossary of Terms.

Assume that the reader is unfamiliar with the field of education. Laypersons, including media professionals, will make up a sizeable portion of the reading audience for many of your reports. It is safe to assume that most of them will be unfamiliar with the terms and programs that you refer to on an everyday basis. To make it easy for them, use a glossary in the front of the report to define terms or explain programs referred to in the report. Avoid esoteric terminology, and do not use abbreviations unless they have been defined in the glossary or are already identified in the report. People, who do not understand the terminology you are using without explanation, will give up reading the report.

Tip Twelve: Have Your Report Read by an Independent Reviewer.

This is the easiest task in producing the final report and one of the most important. As writers we have a tendency to get too close to our work. We may be too familiar with the subject matter or too impressed with our writing style. As a result, sufficient detail may be lacking in the explanation of some findings or too much abstract language used in others. An impartial reader who is aware of the intended audience can help to uncover flaws and alert you to areas where your readers may have difficulties or questions. Also, make sure that your report is "well dressed." The adage that "perception is reality" is true. Typographical errors leave a bad impression and take away from your credibility. In the eyes of the reader, a carelessly compiled report can equate to a negligent and lax school system. If words are misspelled or there are grammatical errors, this can only work against you—regardless of the quality of the report you are presenting. Have a colleague read your report as a critical reviewer before it goes to the public.

Tip Thirteen: Treat the Reading and Listening Audience with Respect and Dignity.

There will be a few who cannot sing your praises enough and a few who cannot sing your praises at all. Think about the people under the normal curve; these two small groups are the "tails." Those who disagree with your findings or criticize some aspect of the study may even border on being petty. As difficult as it may be, the respect and dignity of all consumers of public education must be respected. Listening to what laypersons say, honestly answering questions that you can answer, and finding out information for questions you can't answer go a long way in promoting your school. As the educational leader, this approach is always a win-win even though it is tough-tough.

CONCLUSION

Unlike many fads and trends in public education, data-driven decision making is here to stay. This is because strategic decisions, based on systematically collected and compiled information, make for sound action steps. Yet, the entrance of this data-based approach has its price. It is more work, it is hard work, and it requires a commitment over time. It cannot be undertaken quickly; data warehouses do not sprout up without meticulous input and scrutiny. They need to be managed and updated. Data mining, using the technology and software that abounds, must be selected carefully for each school system's unique information needs. For some schools this purchase is a huge investment and one that they cannot take back to the

store for a refund if they are not pleased a year later. The statistical procedures that are applied to the data sets must be selected carefully, planned
wisely, and executed with at least a basic level of expertise. Statistics must
be interpreted correctly, honestly and reported simply. Reports must make
sense and be easily assimilated by lay audiences. But the price is worth it.
Decisions based on data will represent a gigantic thrust forward in school
reform and improvement for educators and stakeholders alike.

INDEX

ABOUT THE AUTHORS

Susan Rovezzi Carroll, Ph.D., is president of Words & Numbers Research, Inc., a marketing research firm that she founded in 1984. The company provides customized information on which corporations, school systems, hospitals, and other institutions can base strategic decisions. Dr. Carroll has won awards in the areas of leadership, scholarship, and business. A former associate professor at the University of Connecticut's graduate school, she has authored many peer review articles in the field of education and a best-selling book. Dr. Carroll received her doctorate from the University of Connecticut in 1981.

As vice president of Words & Numbers Research, Inc., **David Carroll, M.S.W.,** provides expert help to school systems in program evaluation and strategic planning. He has conducted multi-year assessments for dropout prevention and school-to-work initiatives, remedial education, urban violence prevention, and college placement for low-income students. Mr. Carroll consults extensively in the area of campaign management and has helped with many successful referenda and election victories. Mr. Carroll received his master's degree in Planning and Community Organization from the University of Connecticut in 1977.

WORDS & NUMBERS RESEARCH, INC., COMPANY PROFILE

Words & Numbers Research, Inc., was founded in 1984 by its current president, Susan Carroll, Ph.D. In 1993, the company was chosen by the U.S. Small Business Administration as a successful small business.

During eighteen years of operation, the firm has designed and executed hundreds of studies for diversified clientele. The level of client satisfaction with the quality of the work has been evident by the high rate of referral through word-of-mouth testimonials; the firm does not advertise.

The mail and phone surveys have been qualitative and quantitative, as the name of the firm suggests. Customer satisfaction, new product/service idea testing, brand name awareness, competition analysis, employee evaluation, and image assessment are typical studies performed.

Projects have been conducted for many national and multinational corporations (names of these clients are confidential). The American Dietetic Association, the Connecticut Department of Economic Development Tourism Division, the University of Connecticut Development Office, the Connecticut Department of Education, insurance companies, hospitals, public schools, universities, utility companies, and nursing homes have also used the services of Words & Numbers Research, Inc. The Connecticut Bar Association, with 11,000 consumers, selected Words & Numbers Research, Inc., to survey its members.

wordsnum@snet.net

www.wordsandnumbers.org